loving your
spouse

when you
feel like
walking away

loving your spouse

spouse

when you feel like walking away

REAL HELP FOR DESPERATE HEARTS IN DIFFICULT MARRIAGES

GARY CHAPMAN

NORTHFIELD PUBLISHING

CHICAGO

Edited by Elizabeth Cody Newenhuyse
Interior and cover design: Erik M. Peterson
Cover photo of heart icons copyright © 2016 by Rakdee / iStock (528981422). All rights reserved.
Author photo: P.S. Photography

Library of Congress Cataloging-in-Publication Data

Names: Chapman, Gary D., 1938- author.
Title: Loving your spouse when you feel like walking away : real help for desperate hearts in difficult marriages / Gary Chapman.
Other titles: Desperate marriages
Description: Chicago : Northfield Publishing, [2018] | "This is a revised edition of Desperate Marriages: Moving Toward Hope and Healing in Your Relationship." | Includes bibliographical references. |
Identifiers: LCCN 2017055014 (print) | LCCN 2017057780 (ebook) | ISBN 9780802496423 () | ISBN 9780802418104
Subjects: LCSH: Marriage. | Reconciliation. | Communication in marriage.
Classification: LCC HQ734 (ebook) | LCC HQ734 .C464 2018 (print) | DDC 306.81--dc23
LC record available at https://lccn.loc.gov/2017055014

ISBN: 978-0-8024-1810-4

We hope you enjoy this book from Northfield Publishing. Our goal is to provide high-quality, thought-provoking books and products that connect truth to your real needs and challenges. For more information on other books and products helping you with your most important relationships, go to www.moodypublishers.com or write to:

Northfield Publishing
215 West Locust Street
Chicago, IL 60610

3 5 7 9 10 8 6 4

Printed in the United States of America

To the many couples
who have shared their marital struggles with me
and who have given me the extreme joy
of seeing them take the road to
Reality Living.

Contents

Introduction

I was in a Chicago suburb one cold Saturday morning, leading my "The Marriage You've Always Wanted" seminar, when I first met Maria. Earlier I had given the audience a summary of my book *One More Try: What to Do When Your Marriage Is Falling Apart*. I had encouraged audience members to get a copy for any of their friends who were separated. Maria had purchased the book and was holding it in her hands.

"Dr. Chapman, when are you going to write a book for me?" she asked.

"What do you mean?"

"I'm sure this book is good for those who are contemplating divorce," she said, "but what about people like me? My husband and I are not separated. We have been married for seventeen years. Neither of us believes in divorce; we have strong religious convictions, but our marriage is miserable. We have some really big problems that we have never been able to resolve. We'll fight about them and then make up, and things will be fine for a few weeks. Then we're back into warfare again. We need help.

"We went for counseling one time for a few sessions, but it didn't seem to help. We've read some books on marriage, but they just don't seem to deal with our problems. I know there must be other couples like us who really want their marriages to work but haven't been able to find answers."

I found out later that Maria was living with an alcoholic

husband who, for that and other reasons, was also irresponsible in his work patterns. Thus, finances had been a problem during their entire marriage.

Since my conversation with Maria, I have written several more books, but I have never forgotten her question: "When are you going to write a book for me?" I have had no further contact with her and do not know what has happened in her marriage. But if I could see her again, I would say, "Maria, this one's for you." Yes, for Maria—and for thousands of others like her who sincerely want to make their "miserable" marriages work.

Three factors motivated me to write this book. First, large numbers of people like Maria have approached me at my seminars, asking for practical help with what I (and they) consider to be major barriers to marital unity, the kind of issues that we do not have time to deal with in a weekend seminar—problems that have lingered for years and whose roots run deep; problems that, if they are not solved, can and do destroy many marriages.

The second catalyst for writing this book is the memory of my own struggles in the early years of my marriage. I well remember the pain that followed months of trying to do what I thought was right, yet to no avail. I remember the sense of helplessness that overwhelmed me, the recurring thought that I was married to someone with whom I would never have real intimacy. The problems seemed so deep and my resources so shallow that I found it difficult even to pursue "another approach." But there were answers, and eventually we found them. Karolyn and I have been married for more than fifty years now and have come to experience an intimacy I never dreamed possible. The pain is a distant memory, but it motivates me to help others who struggle as sincerely as we struggled.

The third force that pushed me to write this book is the steady stream of individuals with whom I have worked in the counseling office over the years—people who have had to deal with alcoholism, verbal and physical abuse, the unfaithfulness of a spouse, a controlling personality, or those who have had to deal with a painful past involving child abuse or low self-esteem; others have been married to workaholics, and others to irresponsible mates. One of the rewards of counseling is seeing these kinds of people take responsible steps to deal with genuine problems, to support them in their efforts, and to see the fruit of improved relationships. I am convinced that their successes need a wider audience and that perhaps the steps they took will also give guidance to others.

I have changed their names and enough details to protect their privacy, but the accounts you will read in the following pages depict the lives of real people with real problems who found meaningful solutions in desperate marriages.

In each chapter, I will seek first to identify the nature of the specific problem and draw from social and psychological research where available. In questions of morality, I will offer guidelines from my own Judeo-Christian heritage. In addition, following a number of the chapters, we give you resources for further help.

My intended purpose is to give practical suggestions on how to move your marriage from where it is to where you want it to be. Obviously, I cannot guarantee you success, but I can guarantee you the satisfaction of knowing that you have given your marriage your best effort.

Yes, Maria, this one's for you.

PART 1

when
you're
desperate

1

The Valley of Pain

Thousands of couples are struggling in their marriages. Maybe you are one of them. You could write a book titled *How to Be Married and Miserable*. Some of you have been married for five years and others for twenty-five years. You entered marriage with the same high hopes with which most of us said, "I do." You never intended to be miserable; in fact, you dreamed that in marriage you would be supremely happy. Some of you were happy before you got married and anticipated that marriage would simply enhance your already exciting life. Others entered marriage with a deeply dysfunctional history. Your hope was that in marriage you would finally discover meaning and happiness.

In every case, a man and woman anticipated that marriage would be a road leading upward, that whatever life had been to that point, it would get better after marriage.

Your experience, though, has been that since the mountain-top celebration of the wedding, the road has wound downward. There have been a few peaks of enjoyment and a few curves that offered a promising vista. But the vista later turned out to be a mirage, and the marital road again turned downward. For a long time, you have lived in the valley of pain, emptiness, and frustration. You live in a desperate marriage.

You probably really don't want to divorce. For many of you, religious beliefs discourage you from taking that exit. For others, the children strongly motivate you to keep your marriage together. Still others find enough moments of happiness or support to keep alive your hopes for a better marriage.

You sincerely hope that things will get better. Many of you feel that you have tried to deal with the issues that have kept you and your spouse from marital unity. Most are discouraged with the results. If you have gone for counseling, it has not been very productive. If you have read books, you have read them alone, wishing that your spouse could hear what the distant author is saying and be moved to change. Some of you have tried the calm, cool, straightforward method of gentle confrontation. Your spouse has responded with silence. In desperation some of you have tried yelling and screaming. Your pain has been so intense that you have actually lost control trying to express it. In some cases your loud cries for help have prompted your spouse to launch a counterattack. In other cases your spouse has simply withdrawn.

The problems with which you and other married couples grapple cannot be solved by having a nice chat. Nor do the problems melt under the sunny cheer of pious platitudes. These problems, like cancer, eat away at the vitality of a marriage. The issues vary from couple to couple, but the intensity of the pain runs deep for all.

Through the pages of this book, I will take you behind closed doors into the privacy of my counseling office and let you listen as husbands and wives share their painful situations. I also invite you to listen to what people tell me at the marriage seminars I lead across the country. (I have changed names and details to protect these people.) I urge you to believe that there is hope for your hard marriage.

HOPE FOR THE DESPERATE

In this book I will talk about how to deal with a spouse who is irresponsible or a workaholic; a spouse who is controlling, uncommunicative; verbally, physically, or sexually abusive; unfaithful or depressed; a spouse who is an alcoholic or drug abuser. For all of these situations—and others—you can find solutions that may preserve your marriage.

I am under no illusion that I can provide a magic formula to bring healing to all such marriages. However, I do believe, based on my own experience in counseling, research in the field, and sound moral principles, that there is hope for the hardest of marriages.

I believe that in every troubled marriage, one or both partners can take positive steps that have the potential for changing the emotional climate in a marriage. In due time, spouses can find answers to their problems. For most couples, ultimate solutions will depend not only on their own actions but also on the support of the religious and therapeutic community in their city. But I will say it again: There is hope for lasting solutions in troubled marriages.

ARE YOU A CAPTIVE TO MYTHS?

First, you have to look hard at what you believe—which is a part of what I call practicing *reality living*. Reality living begins by identifying myths that have held you captive. Then it accepts them for what they are—myths, not truths. You can break their bonds as you begin to base your actions on truth rather than myth.

Reality living means that you take responsibility for your own thoughts, feelings, and actions. It requires you to appraise your life situation honestly and refuse to shift the blame for your unhappiness to others.

Look at the following four statements. Answer them honestly with *true* or *false*.

1. My environment determines my state of mind.
2. People cannot change.
3. In a desperate marriage, I have only two options—resigning myself to a life of misery or getting out of the marriage.
4. Some situations are hopeless—and my situation is one of these.

If you answered "true" to any of these statements, please read on. In fact, all four statements are false. Unfortunately, many people in desperate marriages base their lives on these commonly held myths.

Those who accept any of the four myths above will act accordingly, so that their actions become a part of the problem rather than a part of the solution. Let's look at the outcome of accepting and acting on each of these myths.

Myth Number One: My environment determines my state of mind. The commonly held view of our day is that we are all victims of our environment. This myth is expressed in the following statements:

"If I grew up in a loving, supportive family, I will be a loving, supportive person."

"If I grew up in a dysfunctional family, then I am destined to failure in relationships."

"If I am married to an alcoholic husband, I will live a miserable life."

"My emotional state depends on the actions of my spouse."

This kind of approach to life renders anyone helpless in a hostile environment. It prompts feelings of hopelessness and often leads to depression. In a desperate marriage, this victim mentality leads a spouse to conclude, "My life is miserable, and my only hope is the death of my spouse or divorce." Many people daydream of both.

Your environment certainly affects who you are, but it does not control you. Rather than being a helpless victim, you can overcome an environment thick with obstacles, whether blindness (Helen Keller) or polio (Franklin Roosevelt) or racism (too many to name) or an alcoholic parent whose abuse has stayed with you and impacted your marriage. Your environment may influence you, but it need not dictate or destroy your marriage and your life.

Myth Number Two: People cannot change. This myth asserts that once people reach adulthood, personality traits and behavior patterns are set in concrete. Those who believe this myth reason that if a spouse has demonstrated a certain behavior for a long period of time, he or she will continue to act this way.

A wife assumes that her husband, who was sexually active with multiple partners before marriage and sexually unfaithful after marriage, is addicted to this behavior and cannot change.

A husband assumes that his wife, who has been irresponsible in money management for the first fifteen years of marriage, will always be financially irresponsible.

If you accept this myth as truth, you will experience feelings of futility and hopelessness. The fact is, you can go to any library and find biographies of people—adults—who have made radical changes in their behavior patterns. Saint Augustine once lived for pleasure and thought his desires were inescapable. The late Charles Colson, following a conversion while in prison, repented of his wrongdoing in the Watergate scandal and launched an international agency to offer prisoners spiritual help.

People can and do change, and often the changes are dramatic.

Myth Number Three: In a troubled marriage, I have only two options—resigning myself to a life of misery or getting out of the marriage. Those who believe this myth limit their horizons to two equally devastating alternatives and then become a prisoner of that choice. Thousands of people live in self-made prisons because they believe this myth of limited choices.

Shannon and David believed this myth. For fifteen years they experienced misery and contemplated divorce, but as they left my office after six months of counseling, David said, "I used to leave your office with rage in my heart toward Shannon. Today I leave realizing what a wonderful wife I have."

> *Don't simply settle for misery or divorce.*

A smile spread across Shannon's face as she spoke. "Dr. Chapman, I never dreamed that I could love him again and we could have the marriage we have."

Obviously, Shannon and David broke the bonds of this myth. You can do the same. Do not let yourself believe that you have only two options in a desperate marriage. Don't simply settle for misery or divorce.

Myth Number Four: Some situations are hopeless—and my situation is one of these. The person who accepts this myth believes: Perhaps there is hope for others, but my marriage is hopeless. The hurt is too deep. The damage is irreversible. There is no hope. This kind of thinking leads to depression and sometimes suicide.

I listened with tears as Lisa, a thirty-five-year-old mother, shared her story of watching her father murder her mother and then turn the gun on himself. Lisa was ten when she experienced this tragedy. No doubt her father felt his situation was hopeless.

You may have struggled in your marriage for years. You may feel that nothing you have tried has worked. You may even have had people tell you that your marriage is hopeless. Don't let yourself believe that. Your marriage is not beyond hope.

This book will explore the nature of problems in desperate marriages and encourage you to dismiss these myths and take steps toward healing rather than sinking deeper into the misery of such relationships. But first, let's look at what has become a rather popular approach to such major marital problems, namely the exit-marked divorce.

WHY NOT JUST WALK AWAY?

Ours has been called the "Throwaway Society." We buy our food in beautiful containers, which we then throw away. Our cars and tech devices quickly become obsolete. We give our furniture to the secondhand shop not because it is no longer functional, but because it is no longer in style. We even "throw away" unwanted pregnancies. We sustain business relationships only so long as they are profitable to the bottom line. Thus, it is no shock that our society has come to accept the concept of a "throwaway marriage." If you are no longer happy with your spouse, and your relationship has run on hard times, the easy thing is to abandon the relationship and start over.

I wish that I could recommend divorce as an option. When I listen to the deeply pained people in my office and at my seminars, my natural response is to cry, "Get out, get out, get out! Abandon the loser and get on with your life." That would certainly be my approach if I had purchased bad stock. I would get out before the stock fell further. But a spouse is not stock. A spouse is a person— a person with emotions, personality, desires, and frustrations; a person to whom you were deeply attracted at one point in your life; a person for whom you had warm feelings and genuine care. So deeply were the two of you attracted to each other that you made a public commitment of your lives to each other "so long as we both shall live." Now you have a history together. You may even have parented children together.

No one can walk away from a spouse as easily as he or she can sell bad stock. Indeed, talk to most adults who have chosen divorce as the answer, and you will find the divorce was preceded by months of intense inner struggle, and that the whole ordeal is still viewed as a deeply painful experience.

Kristin was sitting in my office two years after her divorce from Dave. "Our marriage was bad," she said, "but our divorce is even worse. I still have all the responsibilities I had when we were married, and now I have less time and less money. When we were married, I worked part-time to help out with the bills. Now I have to work full-time, which gives me less time with the girls. When I am at home, I seem to be more irritable. I find myself snapping at the girls when they don't respond immediately to my requests."

Thousands of divorced moms can identify with Kristin. Divorce doesn't treat them fairly. The stresses of meeting the physical and emotional needs of their children seem overwhelming at times.

Not all who undergo divorce experience such hardship; yet all find the adjustments painful, even when they remarry.

Michael was all smiles when he said to me, "I finally met the love of my life. We're going to get married in June. I've never been happier. She has two kids, and I think they're great. When I was going through my divorce, I never dreamed that I would be happy again. I now believe that I'm about to get my life back on track."

Michael had been divorced for three years at the time of our conversation. However, six months after his marriage to Kelly, he was back in my office, complaining about his inability to get along with Kelly and her children.

"It's like I'm an outsider," he said. "She always puts the kids before me. And when I try to discipline them, she takes their side against me. I can't spend a dime without her approval. I've never been so miserable in my life. How did I let myself get into this mess?" Michael is experiencing the common struggles of establishing a "blended family."

And what about the children who watch their parents divorce? In her book, *Generation Ex*, author and child of multiple divorces Jen Abbas writes candidly:

> As I entered adulthood anticipating my hard-earned independence, I was stunned to discover that my parents' divorces seemed to affect me *more* each year, not less. Even though I was successful academically and professionally, I found myself becoming more insecure each year about my emotional abilities. As I began to see my friends marry, I started to question my ability to successfully create and maintain intimate relationships, especially my own future marriage. I began to see how the marriages—and divorces—of my parents had influenced my relationships, especially when it came to trust. And when it came to love, I was paralyzed because what I wanted so desperately was that which I feared the most.[1]

Through the years I have counseled enough divorced persons to know that while divorce removes some pressures, it creates a host of others. I am not naive enough to suggest that divorce can be eliminated from the human landscape. I am saying, however, that divorce should be the last possible alternative. It should be preceded by every effort at reconciling differences, dealing with issues, and solving problems. Far too many couples in our society have opted for divorce too soon and at too great a price. I believe that many divorced couples could have reconciled if they had sought and found proper help. Thus, the focus of this book about difficult marriages is not on divorce but on something I believe offers far more hope—reality living.

Reality living, which begins by recognizing the myths and continues by rejecting those myths, ends up embracing the positive actions that one individual can take to stimulate constructive change in a relationship. In the next chapter I will give you the basic principles of this approach, and in the following chapters I will show you how to apply these principles to really hard marriages—which, as you will see, take many forms.

2

Where You Start:
Attitude and Actions

When we are deeply unhappy, we can become stuck in our own misery, feeling there is no way out—especially if the situation we're in never seems to change. Yes, it's hard to be positive when you've struggled in a hard marriage for years. It's hard to be positive when we feel as if we are the victim and that our spouse is the one with the problem. At one level, that's true: we are not the alcoholic, we are not the abuser, we are not the irresponsible one.

But we *can* change some things. And if our situation is to change, we first need to deal with *how we think about it*—beginning with moving beyond the myths we identified in the previous chapter. We start by telling ourselves four important truths:

My environment does *not* determine my state of mind.

People *can* change.

In a desperate marriage, I do *not* have only two options—resigning myself to a life of misery or getting out.

My situation is *not* hopeless.

6 REALITIES

But there's more. Let me share six realities—focusing on how we think about ourselves and our marriage—that can start to pull us out of that "no way out" sense of hopelessness.

1. I am responsible for my own attitude. Reality living approaches life with the assumption that we are responsible for our own state of mind. Trouble is inevitable, but misery is optional. Attitude has to do with the way we choose to think about things. It has to do with focus.

Negative thinking tends to beget negative thinking. If you focus on how terrible the situation is, it will get worse. But if you focus on one positive thing in a situation, another will appear. In the darkest night of a miserable marriage, there is always a flickering light. If you focus on that light, it will eventually flood the room.

> *In the darkest night of a miserable marriage, there is always a flickering light.*

Wendy said, "My husband hasn't had a full-time job in three years. The good part is not being able to afford cable TV or Netflix. We've done a lot more talking in the evenings."

She went on to say, "These three years have been tough, but we have learned a lot. Our philosophy has been 'Let's see how many things we can do without—things that everybody else thinks they have to have.' It's amazing how many things you can do without. It's been a challenge, but we are going to make the most of it."

Three weeks after I met Wendy, I encountered Lou Ann. She was at the point of mental and physical exhaustion. Her husband had been out of work for ten months and was working a part-time job while looking for full-time employment.

Lou Ann had been biting her nails for ten months. She was certain that they would lose everything they owned; she decried the fact that they could not afford much in the way of entertainment and talked about how difficult it was to operate with only one car. Every day she lived on the cutting edge of despair.

The difference between Wendy and Lou Ann was basically a matter of attitude. Their problems were very similar, but their attitudes were very different—and that difference had a profound impact on their physical and emotional well-being and, ultimately, their marriages.

This challenge of maintaining a positive mental attitude is not a contemporary idea. It is found clearly in the first-century writings of Saul of Tarsus (who became Paul the apostle): "Do not be anxious about anything, but in every situation, by prayer and petition, with thanksgiving, present your requests to God. And the peace of God, which transcends all understanding, will guard your hearts and your minds. . . . Finally, brothers and sisters, whatever is true, whatever is noble, whatever is right, whatever is pure, whatever is lovely, whatever is admirable—if anything is excellent or praiseworthy—think about such things."[1]

This first postulate of reality living is that I am responsible for my own attitude. The second is closely associated with the first.

2. My attitude affects my actions. If we have a pessimistic, defeatist, negative attitude, we will express it in negative words and behavior. At that point, we become a part of the problem rather than part of the solution.

The reality is that you may not be able to control your environment; you may have to deal with sickness, an alcoholic spouse, a teenager on drugs, a mother who abandoned you, a father who abused you, a spouse who is irresponsible, aging parents, and on and on. You can, however, control your attitude toward your environment. And your attitude will greatly influence your behavior.

Clearly Wendy and Lou Ann demonstrated this reality. With her positive attitude, Wendy did several things to enhance the climate of her marriage. She gave her husband affirming words when he got discouraged in his job search. She assured him that the right job would come, and that in the meantime, they would make it on his part-time job and her freelance career. She suggested that they sell some things on Craigslist to obtain "fun" money. They made enough so that they could occasionally go out to eat and attend a movie or some other recreational activity. Wendy's positive attitude led her to positive, creative actions.

On the other hand, Lou Ann was verbally critical of her husband for ten months. When he came home without a job, she asked him, "What did you do wrong this time?" She told all her friends how disappointed she was in her husband. He often overheard her on the telephone saying such things as: "I don't know what we're going to do if he doesn't get a job soon." Her husband had a part-time job, but she did not. Her reasoning was, "We can't make a living on part-time jobs, so why bother?" She spent most of her time sleeping, watching television, and visiting with her friends. Her marriage was in serious trouble. Her negative attitude led to negative actions, which compounded the problems in her marriage.

I understand that when you have been dealing with a problem for years it becomes harder and harder to muster up a positive attitude and the emotional energy to focus on solutions. Negative thoughts have created deep neurological pathways in the brain. But as humans, we are capable of altering these pathways. Attitude affects actions, and actions influence others. This brings us to the third principle of reality living.

3. I cannot change others, but I can influence others. The two parts of this reality must never be separated. That we cannot change a spouse is a truth we recite often, but we often overlook the truth that we can and do influence a spouse. Because we are individuals and because we have free will, no one can force us to change our thoughts or behavior. On the other hand, because we are relational creatures, others do influence us. Advertisers make millions of dollars each year because of this reality.

So in marriage, you must acknowledge that you cannot change your spouse. You cannot make him or her stop or start certain behaviors. Nor can you control the words that come from your spouse's mouth or the way he or she thinks or feels. You can make requests of your spouse, but you cannot know that he or she will respond positively.

When you fail to understand this reality, you are likely to fall into the trap of manipulating your spouse. The idea behind manipulation is: "If I do this, I will force my spouse to do that." Manipulation may involve positive stimuli: "If I can make my wife happy enough, she will respond to my request." It can also involve negative stimuli: "If I can make my husband miserable enough, he will respond to my request."

All efforts at manipulation will ultimately fail. No one wants to be controlled by a spouse.

Your inability to change your spouse must be laid alongside your very real ability to influence a spouse for better or for worse. All spouses influence each other every day with attitudes and actions.

This means that your spouse's words and behavior may cause you tremendous pain, hurt, or discouragement. But this reality also means that through positive actions and words, you can influence your spouse toward positive change.

Over the years, I have tested this reality with numerous individuals in troubled marriages. When one spouse willingly chooses a positive attitude that leads to positive actions, the change in his or her partner is often radical.

One woman said, "I can't believe what has happened to my husband since I have tried to respond to him with positive words and actions. I never dreamed that he could be as loving and kind as he has been for the last two months. This is more change than I ever anticipated." The reality of the power of positive influence holds tremendous potential for desperate marriages.

I hear you saying, "But, Dr. Chapman, how can I be positive when I am feeling so angry?" Read on for the next reality-living principle.

4. My emotions do not control my actions. In the last several decades, Western society has given an undue emphasis to human emotions. In fact, we have made emotions our guiding star. The search for self-understanding has led us to the conclusion that "I am what I *feel*" and that authentic living is being "true to my feelings."

When applied to a desperate marriage, this philosophy advises, "If I don't have love feelings for my spouse any longer, I should admit it and get out of the marriage. If I feel hurt and angry, I would be hypocritical to say or do something kind to my spouse." This philosophy fails to reckon with the reality that human beings are more than their emotions.

The truth is, you experience life through the five senses: sight, sound, smell, taste, and touch. In response to what you experience through the senses, you have thoughts, feelings, desires. And you take actions.

In your thoughts, you interpret what you experience through the five senses. If you see dirty dishes in the sink at 10:30 p.m., you might interpret that to mean that your spouse is lazy and uncaring.

Emotions will accompany your thoughts. Believing that your spouse is lazy, you may feel disappointment, anger, and frustration.

In response to thoughts and feelings, you have desires. The dirty dishes may fire you up to give your spouse a lecture on irresponsibility: "Why didn't you clean up? I asked you to! And now it's time for bed! Oh, never mind, *I'll* do it . . . " (heavy sigh, clattering).

How do you think your spouse will respond? Cheerfully? Maybe. But probably not. And you won't be feeling so good yourself, angry at bedtime. If, on the other hand, you ask yourself, "*What is the best thing to do in this situation?*" you are far more likely to take positive action. You might, again, decide to clean up yourself—but this time tell your spouse, "I love you so much that I didn't want you to face those dirty dishes in the morning." Or you could decide to simply let it go and not react.

Those who say it is hypocritical to take positive action when they have negative feelings are operating on the assumption that the true self is determined by emotions. I am suggesting that is a false premise, and to the degree that it has permeated Western thinking, it has been detrimental to family relationships.

In other areas of life, you often go against your emotions. For example, if you got out of bed only on the mornings that you "felt" like getting out of bed, you would have bedsores. The fact is, almost every morning, you go against your feelings, get up, do something, and later feel good about having gotten out of bed. The same principle is true in relationships.

You can learn to acknowledge your negative emotions but

> *You can learn to acknowledge your negative emotions but not to follow them.*

not to follow them. You should not deny that you feel disappointed, frustrated, angry, hurt, apathetic, or bitter, but you can refuse to let those emotions control your actions. You can choose the higher road by asking such questions as: *What is best? What is right? What is good? What is loving?* You can allow your actions to be controlled by these noble thoughts. Taking such positive actions holds the potential for bringing healing to a relationship and restoring positive feelings in your marriage.

I am not suggesting that emotions are unimportant. They are indicators that things are going well or not so well in a relationship. But if you understand that negative actions will make things worse and positive actions hold the potential for making things better, you will always choose the high road. Your emotions always influence you, but you do not need to let them control you.

This reality has profound implications for a hard marriage. It means that you can say and do positive things to and for your spouse in spite of the fact that you have strong negative emotions toward them. To take such positive actions does not deny that your marriage is in serious trouble. It means that you choose to take steps that hold *potential for positive change* rather than allowing negative behavior to escalate.

One husband said, "My wife has disappointed me so much and hurt me so deeply that I have no desire to do anything good for her." He is stating clearly his emotional state and his lack of desire for positive action. He was not being hypocritical when he added, "But understanding the power of positive actions, I will choose to wash and vacuum her car because I know that is something she would like for me to do."

One positive action does not heal the hurt of a lifetime, but it is a step in the right direction. A series of positive actions holds the potential for turning the tide in a troubled marriage.

5. Admitting my imperfections does not mean that I am a failure. Most miserable marriages include a stone wall between husband and wife, built over many years. Each stone represents an event in the past where one of them has failed the other. These are the things people talk about when they sit in the counseling office. The husband complains, "She has been critical of my performance on the job and as a father. . . . She never says anything positive about what I do, and she puts me down in front of the kids."

On the other hand, she gripes, "He is married to his job—even when he comes home, he's in his home office catching up or watching sports on TV. He doesn't help around the house and hardly gives me the time of day."

Many times one spouse is more at fault than the other, but the fact is that neither has been perfect.

The list goes on and on. Each spouse recounts what the other has done to make the marriage miserable. This wall stands as a monument to self-centered living, and it's a barrier to marital intimacy.

Demolishing this emotional wall is essential for rebuilding a desperate marriage. Destroying the wall requires both individuals to admit that they are imperfect and have failed each other. I am not implying that the responsibility for the wall is equally distributed between the husband and the wife. Many times, one is more at fault than the other, but the fact is that neither spouse has been perfect.

To acknowledge your imperfections does not mean you are a failure; it is an admission that you are human. As humans, you and I have the potential for loving, kind, and good behavior, but we also have the potential for self-centered, destructive behavior. For all of us, our marital history is a mixed bag of good and bad behavior. Admitting past failures and asking for forgiveness is one of the most liberating of all human experiences.

When you admit your failures and request forgiveness, you begin tearing the wall down on your side. Your spouse may readily forgive you or may be reluctant to do so, but you have done the most positive thing you can do about past failures. You cannot remove them, nor can you remove all their results, but you can acknowledge them and request forgiveness.

I am fully aware that most of the people who read this book will read it alone.

Many people have found the following statements to be helpful in verbalizing their confession of past failures:

"I've been thinking about us, and I realize that in the past I have not been the perfect husband/wife. In many ways I have failed you and hurt you. I am sincerely sorry for these failures. I hope that you will be able to forgive me for these. I sincerely want to be a better husband/wife. And with God's help, I want to make the future different."

Whether your spouse verbalizes forgiveness or has some less enthusiastic response, you have taken the first step in tearing down the wall between the two of you. If the hurt has been deep, your spouse may question your sincerity. He or she may even say, "I've heard that line before," or "I'm not sure that I can forgive you." Whatever the response, you have planted in his or her mind the idea that the future is going to be different. If, in fact, you begin to make positive changes as a spouse, the day may come when your partner will freely forgive past failures.

To admit your own past failures does not mean that you are accepting all the responsibility for the problems in your marriage. It does mean that you are no longer using your spouse's failures as an excuse for your own failures. You are stepping up to take full responsibility for your own failures, and you are doing the most responsible thing you can do by acknowledging your failures and asking forgiveness. In so doing, you are paving the road of hope for a new future.

I am fully aware that most of the people who read this book will read it alone. In a desperate marriage, it is unrealistic to think that husband and wife will sit down together and work through a book. That may happen in a healthy marriage but not in a deeply troubled marriage. Therefore, if you are reading this book, I want to encourage you to tear down the wall on your side. You may feel that the bulk of the wall is on your spouse's side, and that may be true. But the reality is that you cannot tear down his or her wall; you can only tear down the wall on your side. However small it may be, this is a step in the right direction. It lets your spouse know that you are consciously thinking about your marriage relationship.

And now we move on to consider the power of love, the sixth reality-living principle.

6. Love is the most powerful weapon for good in the world. Most of the couples who sit in my office talk about the lack of love, affection, and appreciation they have received from a spouse through the years. Their emotional love tanks are empty, and they are pleading for love. I am deeply sympathetic with this need. I believe love is humanity's deepest emotional need. The difficulty in a desperate marriage is that spouses focus on receiving love rather than giving love. Many husbands say, "If she would just be a little more affectionate, then I could be responsive to her. When she gives me no affection, I just want to stay away from her." He is waiting for love before he loves. However, someone must take the initiative.

The final principle of reality living declares love to be the most powerful weapon for good, and that especially applies in marriage. The problem for many husbands and wives is that they have thought of love as an emotion. In reality, love is an attitude, demonstrated with appropriate behavior. It affects the emotions, but it is not in itself an emotion. Love is the attitude that says, "I choose to look out for your interests. How may I help you?" Then love is expressed in behavior.

The fact that love is an attitude rather than an emotion means that you can love your spouse even when you do not have warm emotional feelings for him or her. That is why in the first century, Paul the apostle wrote to husbands, "Love your wives, just as Christ loved the church and gave himself up for her [by willingly dying on a cross]."[2] In another of his letters, Paul challenged the older women to "urge the younger women to love their husbands."[3] Love can be learned because it is not an emotion.

SPEAKING YOUR SPOUSE'S LOVE LANGUAGE

Part of the problem spouses have in demonstrating love to one another is that they fail to understand that they speak different "love languages." After many years of counseling, I am convinced there are only five basic languages of love. They are:

Words of Affirmation
Verbally affirming your spouse for the good things he or she does

Quality Time
Giving your spouse undivided attention

Receiving Gifts
Presenting a gift to your spouse that says, "I was thinking about you."

Acts of Service
Doing something for your spouse that is meaningful to him or her

Physical Touch
Kissing, embracing, patting on the back, holding hands, having sexual intercourse

Seldom do a husband and wife have the same love language. By nature, you tend to speak your own language. For example, if quality time makes you feel loved, then that's what you try to give your spouse. But if that is not his or her primary language, it will not mean to your spouse what it would mean to you.

So you need to know, and then speak, your spouse's primary love language.

This simple concept, which I have shared in marriage seminars and the book *The 5 Love Languages,* has helped millions of couples.[4] Discovering your spouse's primary love language and choosing to speak it on a regular basis has tremendous potential for changing the emotional climate of your marriage.

Love is the most powerful weapon for good not only in the world but especially in a desperate marriage. When you choose to reach out with a loving attitude and loving actions toward your spouse in spite of past failures, you create a climate where the two of you can resolve conflicts and confess wrongs. A marriage can be reborn. Reality living says, "I will choose the road of love because its potential is far greater than the road of hate."

These six realities hold tremendous potential for desperate marriages. In the chapters that follow, we will look at examples of deeply troubled marriages and listen in on husbands and wives who have applied these reality-living principles and found healing.

I am sympathetic to those who feel that there is no hope for their marriage. But let's not assume that past failures must be repeated in the future. With a new set of guidelines and a willingness to take action, there is hope for a hard marriage.

I understand that you wish your spouse would join you in working on the marriage. That is probably an unrealistic hope at the moment, but that does not mean that your marriage is hopeless. One person must always take the initiative. Perhaps that person will be you.

Why Did
He Do That?

We've dismissed the myths and put the six reality-living principles into action. Now it's time to look at the *why* behind both your and your spouse's behavior.

It's likely that your spouse's negative behavior has been a big part of your hard marriage. Understanding the motivation and impulses behind your spouse's unreasonable, illogical, hurtful, and often destructive behavior may give you helpful insight as you seek to take a new approach to your life and marriage. But equally important is to try to understand why *you* do what you do. As one woman, married for many years, said, "Why do I always become emotional and overreact when my husband does things that always bother me? I know better. It doesn't help. But . . . "

Most human behavior is motivated by what psychologists call "the hidden self." Our motives are hidden from most observers and many close friends, even a spouse. Behavior that is motivated by internal physical needs is probably the easiest to observe and understand. When we are having difficulty breathing, we will drop everything in search of air. When the body is too cold, we find ourselves searching for heat, and when the body is too hot, we search for cool air. But behavior motivated by psychological or spiritual needs is much harder to recognize. Yet understanding such behavior, and the basic needs that motivate the behavior, is crucial for helping your spouse and your marriage.

MEETING A NEED?

Like the woman above who wondered why she always reacted emotionally to her husband's perceived negative behavior, we may not always understand our own inner motivations for what we do. Then how can we possibly understand someone else's behavior? We can't, at least not totally. But we can make educated guesses. What is important is to know that all of your spouse's behavior is motivated by some internal desire or need.

Psychiatrist William Glasser says, "Everything we do—good or bad, effective or ineffective, painful or pleasurable, crazy or sane, sick or well, drunk or sober—is done to satisfy powerful forces within ourselves."[1] This is Glasser's way of saying that even inappropriate behavior serves some function. In some distorted way, such behavior is meeting a psychological need.

The closer you can come to understanding the internal motivation for your spouse's behavior, the better equipped you will be to serve as an agent of positive change in your marriage. If you can help your spouse meet his or her needs in a healthier manner, then you may well see your spouse's behavior change in a positive direction.

Adam complained to me that the biggest trouble in his marriage was that his wife tried to control him. "She thinks she's smarter than I am. It's her arrogant attitude that makes me so angry," he said. His wife, Jessi, explained her perspective: "Any time I disagree with him and share my opinion, he thinks I'm trying to control him. I don't want to control him; I just want to be a part of the decision." This battle had gone on for years before Adam and Jessi came to my office.

We explored the motivation behind Jessi's behavior. It took a while, but Adam did finally realize that indeed his wife's motivation was not to control him but simply to partner with him—to function as a wife rather than as a child. She wanted Adam to have the benefit of her input on the topic of discussion. She was not trying to force him to agree with her; she simply wanted to sense that her ideas were important to him.

When Adam began to understand these motives, his entire response to Jessi changed. He no longer became defensive, angry, and argumentative. He even began to welcome her input. How did this influence Jessi's behavior? Her screaming and name-calling stopped. She no longer had to use such antics to get her husband's attention.

This chapter will not offer an exhaustive list of the inner psychological and spiritual needs that motivate human behavior. Instead, I want to describe a few of the primary inner drives, needs, and desires that often motivate our behavior. I am using the words *needs*, *drives*, and *desires* as synonyms, all describing those inner compulsions that motivate us to take action. I am also using the words *psychological* and *spiritual* to describe those nonphysical needs that so profoundly affect our inner sense of well-being.

THE NEED FOR LOVE

First, and in my opinion most fundamental, is the need to love and be loved. We all feel good about ourselves when we are helping others. This desire to love others accounts for the charitable, altruistic side of human beings. On the other hand, much of our behavior is motivated by our desire to receive love. You feel loved when you have the sense that people genuinely care for you, that your well-being is important to them, that they are looking out for your interests and giving of themselves for your well-being.

This kind of love is the opposite of loneliness. If you feel loved by your spouse, you have the sense of closeness or intimacy, but if you feel you've received little love—if your love tank is empty— you may feel cut off and alone.

Joe has learned from experience that when he speaks kindly to his wife, she tends to reciprocate with loving words and acts toward him. So his words are motivated at least in part by his own need for love.

Abby, on the other hand, complains that her husband, Zack, does not give her enough time. She often raises her voice and delivers angry lectures to him, accusing him of not caring for her. Why does Abby repeatedly berate Zack? It is her effort to try to meet her need for love. Perhaps it has been successful in the past. Perhaps it will be successful in the future, but almost everyone agrees that it is inappropriate and negative behavior.

If you feel your love tank is empty, you may feel cut off and alone.

We must realize that much of our behavior, positive and negative, appropriate and inappropriate, is motivated by an effort to meet our need for love.

THE NEED FOR FREEDOM

Then there is the need for freedom. We desire to order our own lives and not be controlled by another. We want to choose how we live our lives. In a marriage, we want to be free to express our feelings, thoughts, and desires. We want to be free to choose the goals that we will pursue. We want the freedom to read and write what satisfies us, to watch the TV programs in which we have an interest.

This desire for freedom is so strong that whenever you feel that your spouse is trying to manipulate or control you, you tend to become defensive and angry. Your sense of well-being about your marriage dissipates, and you have an awareness that your relationship is not healthy. Your marriage is not likely to return to a state of equilibrium as long as you have the sense that your spouse is trying to control you.

It will be obvious to most that the need for freedom and the need for love are often in conflict. This is why some men are hesitant to marry. They are wonderful lovers so long as their relationship is at the dating stage, but they are reluctant to make the commitment to marriage because they fear this will remove their freedom. A married man may move out of a marriage in search of freedom, but soon he finds himself lonely and seeking love.

If you and your spouse do not find the balance between love and freedom, you will never have a satisfying marriage. To find the balance between meeting these two needs requires give-and-take. You must both learn to give love and give freedom if you expect to receive love and freedom.

Freedom is never without boundaries. Freedom is never absolute; to be totally free is to live a life without love. If you are governed only by your own desires and give no consideration to others, you will soon be in bondage to your desires. Giving your spouse freedom to choose to spend an evening watching a sports event or a dramatic production is far different from giving your spouse freedom to have a relationship with a member of the opposite sex. The idea of "open marriage," which allows each marriage partner to have intimate relationships with others, has never proven to be a functional form of marriage for one simple reason: It violates true love. I'm sure that you do not want your spouse to have that kind of freedom, nor should you demand it for yourself. On the other hand, I'm also sure you do not want to be controlled in every area of life by your spouse. Such control also violates love.

Adam's outbursts at Jessi were motivated by his need for freedom. He perceived that she was trying to control him; therefore, his angry behavior attempted to throw off that control and pursue freedom. When he realized that Jessi was not, in fact, trying to control him, his angry outbursts ceased.

Jordan has been encouraging his wife, Lindsey, to lose weight. He has said it often enough and strongly enough that she now feels that he is trying to control her. In addition, she feels that he does not love her as she is. One night, he again brings up the subject, and she unloads her fiery cannon of flaming words, accusing Jordan of not loving her and trying to control her.

What motivated nice, calm Lindsey to exhibit such explosive behavior? Maybe it was her need for love and her need for freedom. Did her behavior meet her needs? Perhaps she will fulfill her need for love if thirty minutes later Jordan comes in, apologizes, verbally assures her of his love, tenderly embraces her, and assures her that it is not his desire to control her. And if Jordan doesn't mention her weight again for at least six months, then perhaps Lindsey's angry behavior served to meet her need for freedom.

Was Lindsey's behavior positive, appropriate, constructive? The answer is no. Did it meet her needs? The answer is yes, at least momentarily.

One of the tasks in a maturing marriage is to learn to meet

your needs in a mature and wholesome manner and to help your spouse discover the same.

THE NEED FOR SIGNIFICANCE

A third need that motivates much of our behavior is our need for significance. Within each of us rests the desire to do something bigger than ourselves, to accomplish something that will impact the world, something that will give us a sense of fulfillment and satisfaction. This need often motivates altruistic behavior. It is sometimes behind the driven nature of the workaholic. Much of human behavior is motivated by this desire to make a significant impact on the world, something for which we will be remembered.

Many times this drive for significance is heightened by childhood experiences. If Greg tells his son Eric that he will never amount to anything and makes Eric feel that his efforts are never quite enough, Eric may spend a lifetime trying to prove his father wrong and thus obtain significance. He may become a workaholic.

Understanding your spouse's need for significance will greatly enhance your efforts at strengthening your marriage if you are married to a workaholic. We will talk more about this in a later chapter.

THE NEED FOR RECREATION

A fourth need we each have is for recreation or relaxation. Physically, mentally, and emotionally, humans are designed with the need for rhythm of movement between work and play. The old saying "All work and no play makes Jack a dull boy" reflects this fundamental need. This is readily observed by a candid look at our lifestyle. We invest much time and money in play. Take an inventory of the sports equipment—or electronic devices or fancy kitchen gadgets—in your own house, and you will likely find an array of costly signs of this reality.

The men and women who play on the professional sports teams of our nation may be working, but the thousands who watch them are playing. We are unwinding from a stress-filled week. We are enjoying a time with friends; we are socializing, laughing, and relaxing. We are avid in our desire to have fun.

Look at your own behavior and the behavior of your spouse, and you will see that at least some of it is motivated by this desire for recreation and relaxation. The methods of meeting this need are myriad and reflect our unique preferences, but all of us look forward to the fun times of life in which we can relax and enjoy the things and relationships that we have accumulated.

Within each of us rests the desire to do something bigger than ourselves.

Why does Bill come home, click on the TV, and enjoy his favorite drink before engaging in conversation with his wife, Tess? Because he wants to relax before he faces the stress of relating to her. Consciously or unconsciously, he is seeking to meet his need for relaxation. Tess may interpret this behavior as lack of love for her, but if she understands Bill's motivation, perhaps she can find a way to get the love she needs and still allow him the freedom to meet his own needs. She too must find her own way of relaxing, or she will lose her inner psychological equilibrium.

THE NEED FOR PEACE WITH GOD

Then there is what I call the need for peace with God. This is at the center of each person's inner self. The thousands of volumes that deal with religious and spiritual issues testify to the depth of this need. Modern human beings may reject organized religion, but they have not abandoned their search for spiritual reality. On occasion even the avowed atheist will be found Googling "psychics" on the internet, watching the TV evangelist after midnight, or sitting in a silent corner reading the writings of some ancient or modern mystic. There is something within all of us that reaches out to make connection with the nonphysical world. We have not been able to eradicate this need with modern scientific dogmas. In fact, much of human behavior is motivated by this search for peace with God.

Traci was incredulous at her husband Todd's recent interest in studying the Bible. She said to me with fire in her eyes, "I don't understand this, and I don't like it. He spends two or three nights a week reading the Bible and working through a study guide a friend gave him. He has even asked me to attend the Bible study with him. This is a man who has been an atheist since the tenth grade. In college, he made fun of Christians and often took pleasure in debating them. He assured me before we got married that religion would never be a part of our lives, and now he is becoming a fundamentalist Bible freak. Explain that to me."

I didn't sense that Traci was open to an explanation at that moment, and I was deeply sympathetic with her frustration at this sudden turn of events in her husband. But I was certain that Todd was on a search for peace with God. His behavior was motivated by his inner need for a spiritual dimension to his life.

Philosophers and world religious leaders have always seen human beings as possessing a nonmaterial dimension. Blaise Pascal, the French philosopher, said, "The most important thought that ever occupied my mind is that of my individual responsibility to God."[2]

We all have a spiritual hunger that impels us to seek meaning beyond the world of food, sex, and activities. We have a need to find peace with God.

WHAT NOW?

These are examples of the kind of inner psychological-spiritual needs that motivate much of human behavior.

If you and your spouse are to understand each other, you must ask the questions: "What motivates my spouse's behavior? What needs is he or she consciously or subconsciously trying to meet? What motivates my own behavior? What needs am I trying to meet?" As you answer those questions, you will be more able to understand human behavior.

Your method for discovering motivations may involve studying books on human nature, which explore human beings' basic needs. It may involve overtly asking questions of your spouse. Looking at your own inner motivations may also give you clues as to what is behind your spouse's behavior. Hopefully, as you read the illustrations in this book, you will be able to see parallels in your marriage.

None of these approaches will give you exact answers, but they all may help you make an educated guess about the motivation behind your spouse's troublesome behavior. It is understanding this inner motivation that will enlighten you to take actions designed to stimulate constructive change in your spouse's behavior.

In the following chapters, we will seek to apply the principles discussed in these first three chapters. We will look at how the inner needs we just discussed affect marriage.

We will also discuss how reality-living principles can help you take positive action in a desperate marriage. Once more, consider those principles.

I will take you behind closed doors as we look at married

couples and explore the characteristics of various desperate marriages. We will examine the actions of other husbands and wives who have dismissed the myths, acted on reality-living principles, and begun to understand their internal motivations.

These stories may not exactly match your own, but hopefully they will be close enough to give you insights and ideas on positive steps that you can take in seeking to bring about positive change in your marriage.

PART 2

Apathetic
Spouses

4

The
Irresponsible
Spouse

When you entered marriage, you probably assumed you were marrying a responsible person. You assumed that your spouse would carry their part of the load. You knew that your responsibilities might be somewhat different, but you assumed that you would both use your minds and skills for the benefit of the marriage.

After a few years or maybe a few months of marriage, you may have discovered that your spouse is not the responsible person you thought you married. You may feel let down, angry, hurt, betrayed. *It's just not fair,* you may think. *I have to do so much. Why can't he?* Or you may reason, *I don't think I'm expecting too much. I just want her to do her fair share.* If your spouse's irresponsible behavior continues over a long period of time, you will find yourself in a desperate marriage.

For the ten years of Dan and Michelle's marriage, the longest time Dan had held a job was eighteen months. His job problems varied. Sometimes he got into a fight with a fellow employee and simply walked off the job. Other times, he got frustrated with the job or the people he worked with and simply went home one evening and never returned. Between jobs, he often went weeks—and sometimes months—without work. He spent his time sleeping late, watching television, and working out at the local gym.

On the other hand, Michelle had worked a full-time job all ten years of their marriage, except for brief times surrounding the births of their two children. When Dan had a job, he helped her with the bills, but when he was out of work, she carried the whole load.

The tears were flowing freely when Michelle said, "Dr. Chapman, I don't know how much longer I can go on like this."

Like Michelle, Becky also had a troubled marriage, but unemployment was not the issue. Both she and her husband, David, held full-time jobs while rearing three children during their fifteen years of marriage.

Becky's complaint was David's passive lifestyle. "He takes no initiative to do anything around the house. Our bedroom has needed painting for six years. Over and over he says, 'I'll get around to it,' but he never does. The kids' bicycles stay broken for months before he finally gets around to fixing them. Our money sits in a passbook savings account, and he will take no initiative to try to discover an investment where we can get a better return. In the summer, the yardwork never gets done. I'm ashamed to have my friends come by. In fact, last summer I finally hired someone to mow the lawn every week.

"He spends his time on social media and playing online games. I've tried everything I know. I've tried calmly discussing the matter with him. I've tried screaming at him. I've tried ignoring the problem. I've tried being overly kind to him. Nothing seems to make a difference. I don't know what else to do."

Jamal waited until he was thirty-nine before he married. He prided himself on being a bachelor; however, Suzanne swept him off his feet. The top salesperson in her company for the past two years, she was attractive, playful, and deeply in love with Jamal. She also had a five-year-old daughter by a previous marriage. Jamal was her ideal man. She had dreamed of marrying a man who wanted a stay-at-home wife. She wanted to leave the work-force and devote her energies to raising her child. She also hoped to have other children. Jamal was her man, they both agreed.

The first year of marriage was almost perfect. Suzanne contin-ued to work so that they could get the condo and furniture they both wanted. And by the end of the year, they both agreed it was time for her to quit work. They were both excited about reaching this goal, but that's when the problems started. Seven years later, I met a very frustrated husband. Jamal complained that when he arrived home in the afternoon, he had to shovel his way through the house. He could not imagine how the place could be in such disarray in only one day or why Suzanne could not arrange to have things "in order" before he arrived home. His other com-plaint was that she did not cook dinner for him. She fed the kids, but most of the time he had to find his own food.

"Sometimes I have to turn around and go to McDonald's after I get home. I don't understand why she can't keep at least the basics in the house," he said.

"I was happy for her to quit work. I knew that was something she wanted to do, but I thought that if she was going to stay at home, she would at least keep the house clean and cook dinner for me. I don't mind going out one or two evenings a week, but this is too much." He had complained to Suzanne for years, but she had not changed. Jamal felt he was married to an irresponsible

> *Their emotions said, "Get out." Yet they did not want to give up on their marriages.*

wife. Suzanne's irresponsibility created a barrier to marital intimacy.

Michelle, Becky, and Jamal all felt frustrated, hurt, angry, resentful, and miserable. They felt that they had tried, really tried, to work out their marital problems. They realized that their efforts had not always been positive and that, in fact, sometimes their efforts had compounded the problem. But they all were sincere in their efforts. When they arrived in my office, they had little hope. Their emotions said, "Get out." Some of their friends had offered the same recommendation. Yet, for various reasons, they did not want to give up on their marriages.

Let me share with you the approach I took in helping these people become agents of positive change when seemingly irresponsible behaviors threatened their marriages.

WHAT IS THE REAL PROBLEM?

If you are to become an agent of positive change in your marriage, you must first clarify the problem. You must make sure that the problem really is lack of responsibility.

Michelle, Becky, and Jamal all complained that their spouses were irresponsible. Was this really the case? Realize that your perception of reality is always colored by your own personality, values, and desires. Sometimes what you perceive is not objective reality.

Now let's consider Becky's husband's supposed irresponsibility. David had one very responsible job and was a good provider for the family. Becky's concern was that he took no initiative in other areas of the marriage. He was not irresponsible in all areas of life, only in the areas of house maintenance and repair, financial management, and yardwork—but all these were important to Becky.

Suzanne was also an extremely responsible person in one area—mothering. She loved being a stay-at-home mom and spent hours with her two children. She could have gotten the "Creative Mother of the Year" award for the kind of educational experiences she gave her kids. She had demonstrated her ambition before marriage by being the number one salesperson for her company. Now she was turning her energies toward parenting. Keeping the house in order was not high on her priority list, although she did work at making the house safe for the children. She took care of the kids' meals, but when it came to her husband she thought, *Jamal's an adult, and his schedule is unpredictable. He can take care of himself.* She could not understand his concern. "We had agreed that I would stay home with the kids," she said. "I think I'm doing a good job. Why is he upset?"

Michelle had a harder road, married to a husband who was basically irresponsible in all areas of life, not helping with financial provision, not doing much with the kids, not helping with household tasks.

Three couples, three different problems. Thus their actions, designed to spark positive change, will need to be different.

WHERE DOES THE PROBLEM COME FROM?

It always helps to understand something of what is going on in the mind of your spouse. You are not likely to take the right actions without this insight. Let's assume that your husband really has little ambition. He won't work in the home or out of the home, or perhaps he has a regular job to which he is faithful but will do nothing but watch sports or work out in his off hours. He shows no interest in fathering or being a husband. What lies behind this seeming lack of ambition? Understanding the source of his behavior is a part of finding the cure. Let me suggest four possible sources.

First, he may be following the model of his father. Look at his father's lifestyle. Is your husband simply doing what he learned from his dad? Many men enter marriage and repeat the husband/father style that they have observed in their own fathers.

Second, your husband may be rebelling against the model of his father. Maybe his father was a workaholic, and he was never there for his son. His mother often complained about his father's work. So, as a young man, the husband decided that work was bad and that he would never repeat his father's mistakes.

Many of us are keenly aware of our parents' failures. Some of us consciously or subconsciously are trying hard to be different. We do not want to repeat the mistakes of our parents. Often these efforts lead us to the other extreme. The son of a workaholic father may "overcorrect" and become irresponsible in his work patterns. The daughter of a promiscuous mother may become rigid in her attitudes toward sex.

A third possibility is that your husband may have developed a self-centered attitude. At the root of many unambitious spouses is pure and simple selfishness. Perhaps his parents gave him few responsibilities growing up. He developed the mindset that the world owes him a living, and sooner or later the world will deliver. He is a taker but not a giver. He has never learned to provide for others. He expects others to provide for him.

Fourth, your husband's behavior may be an expression of his

resentment toward you. Whatever you want, he will lean in the opposite direction. If you are asking him to do things around the house, he will put them off because in his mind you do not deserve his help. He will likely see your requests as nagging or criticism. His only assertiveness is in making sure that he does not do anything you request. In some area of life, he does not feel that you are meeting his needs. His lack of responsibility toward you is designed to draw attention to his own unmet needs.

These are not the only possibilities, but they are four common sources of irresponsibility. The more clearly you can understand the source of your spouse's irresponsibility, the more likely you are to determine positive steps that you can take to spur constructive change. It is helpful to remember that much of our behavior is motivated by our inner emotional needs—for *love, freedom, significance, recreation,* and *peace with God* (discussed in chapter 3).

> *At the root of many unambitious spouses is pure and simple selfishness.*

Dan: in search of affirmation

What about Dan? In further conversations with Michelle, I discovered that he was suffering from a severe case of insecurity and low self-esteem. He grew up with an alcoholic father who often told him that he would never amount to anything, who regularly criticized him and put down his efforts. Dan had shared all of this with Michelle when they were dating. He was attracted to her because she gave him positive affirmation. She told him how wrong his father was. Finally, Dan had met someone who believed in him and loved him. He responded by doing things that pleased her. He sent her flowers and romantic text messages, something she had always associated with love. It is not hard to understand how the two of them fell in love.

When Michelle and Dan were married, he had been working at the same place for the entire year they dated, so she had no way of knowing before the wedding that during the first ten years of their marriage his employment record would be so erratic; nor did she understand the depth of his anger at his father, which led him to sharp words and critical comments to fellow employees. And with each successive job loss, Michelle became less supportive and more critical.

So Dan sank into depression as his once-loving wife seemed to have joined the voice of his father in condemning him. He had, in fact, come to believe that he was a loser.

The source of Dan's irresponsible behavior was that his need for significance was not being met, and the love that Michelle had given him initially had now dried up. His employment record and his depressed behavior stemmed from his need for self-esteem and love, but that is not what his wife saw. What she saw was his irresponsible behavior, and what she felt was lack of love. Dan had not been meeting her own need for love and support, and her response, out of her own pain, had been to criticize him for his irresponsibility.

David: seeking a positive word

Becky discovered something quite different in her husband. David was very successful in his job and was encouraged because the rewards fed his self-esteem. But he felt his need for love was not being met in the marriage. His response was to draw back from his wife. His primary love language was words of affirmation, but increasingly he heard criticism about spending so much time with social media and doing so little to help her and the children. It seemed to him that Becky seldom gave him a positive word. His love tank was empty, and his irresponsible behavior was shouting, "I will not respond to the requests of one who is not loving me." In turn, Becky became more critical and less loving.

His irresponsible behavior was shouting, "I will not respond to the requests of one who is not loving me."

Thus, the trouble in their relationship had compounded over the years. When Becky began to understand what was happening inside David, she began to get a new perspective on how she could become an agent of positive change in their marriage.

Suzanne: resenting Jamal's control

When Jamal began to focus on the source of Suzanne's behavior, he discovered that she still had a lot of guilt over taking her daughter through a divorce. Before her marriage to him, she had focused her attention on her daughter. She was excelling in her sales job, but with all of her free time she was seeking to enrich her daughter's life. After she was able to become a stay-at-home mom, and after she and Jamal had their own child, she was even more determined to be a good mother.

By the time she married Jamal, her sense of self-worth was strong. She had been a successful career woman. She was now ready to succeed in another area—parenting. Jamal's well-paying vocation enabled her to do this. She was well on her way until he started complaining about her lack of housekeeping and cooking. She felt he was being unfair and was failing to recognize the value of her spending time with the children. When his complaints continued, she felt he was trying to control her life. He was trying to steal her freedom. She refused to buckle to his demands and resolved that neither he nor anyone else would keep her from investing time with her children. He was no longer affirming her self-worth, and in time she felt he no longer loved her. This made it even more difficult for her to be responsive to his demands. This insight set Jamal on a whole new course of action, which brings us to the third and most important consideration.

Jamal and Suzanne: "I think we both need and deserve more from each other"

Jamal was now ready to take action. He realized that he was responsible for his own attitude. If he looked for the positive, he would find it. He discovered that attitudes affect actions and that if he chose to believe there were solutions, he would seek those solutions and take positive steps in the right direction. Although he could not change Suzanne's behavior, Jamal understood that he could influence her by his positive actions—even while his emotions were negative.

Jamal also knew that he had made many mistakes in his efforts to change Suzanne. He was now willing to admit those mistakes and realized that in so doing, he was not admitting that he was a failure, nor was he taking all the blame for their problems.

He was not certain that he could verbalize his thoughts to Suzanne, so he decided to write her a letter. His letter went something like this:

Dear Suzanne,

I've been thinking about us for the past few days. I realize that for a long time, I've been very hard on you. I've been wrong. I love you. Forgive me for getting on your case all the time.

Baby, I've been so proud of you, of what you did in your career. I know I should be proud of you for all that you're doing for our kids. I don't think there could be a better mother. I guess I've just felt a little left out of your love, and maybe that's why I criticize. I know that doesn't excuse it. I know that you're not feeling much love from me either. I think we both need and deserve more from each other.

I know that I want to make the future different. I want to feel close to you again, and I want to be a better dad. My dad wasn't there, and I have a lot to learn about being a father, but I want to be what my kids need and what you need. Let's talk about it. I love you very much.

JAMAL

Jamal and Suzanne talked a week later, at lunch after church while Suzanne's mom watched the children. Jamal wisely asked his wife to give him one suggestion every two weeks; he knew that he could not change everything all at once, but he thought this might be a good way to get started. She agreed, saying, "Sure, I can help—if you really mean it." Her first suggestion was that when he came home at night, rather than making comments about the house, he should find each of the kids, give them a big hug, and spend a few minutes of quality time with each child. Then she wanted him to find her, give her a hug and kiss, and they would spend five minutes sharing with each other the kind of day they had. Jamal was willing to take this step and, in fact, seldom missed a day.

Suzanne continued to give a suggestion every two weeks, and Jamal continued to respond. After two months, he asked her, somewhat cautiously, "How do you think I'm doing?"

As a response, she put her arms around him, kissed him, and said, "Amazing! I love it! You're the best!" It had been a long time since Jamal had heard such affirming words.

He continued to take Suzanne's suggestions seriously. Most of the things she requested he was able to do. He started taking the kids to the local gym once a week. On Saturdays, he sent Suzanne off to see a movie with friends or to go to the spa for some pampering.

Before six months had rolled around, Suzanne had decided that she would like to start receiving a suggestion from Jamal every two weeks on how she could be a better wife. Jamal could not believe his ears, but he agreed. Before the year was out, Suzanne was tutoring a neighbor high school student in business math for an hour each afternoon in exchange for the girl watching the children for forty-five minutes while Suzanne "cleaned up for Jamal." He was shocked when he walked into the house the first afternoon. After three days of this, he knew something was up, so he asked what was going on. She told him about her tutoring plan. He was incredulous that she would go to that much trouble to do something that he had not yet been bold enough to request. She was also cooking dinner Monday, Wednesday, and Friday nights; Tuesdays and Thursdays they went out to eat, and Saturdays and Sundays were free-for-all.

What sparked this positive change in her behavior? Jamal's understanding of Suzanne's inner needs and a willingness to change his own behavior. He backed off from seeking to control her behavior, thus giving her freedom. He began to give her affirming words for her mothering skills, which built her self-esteem and sense of significance. He began to express love in ways that she requested, giving himself to make life easier for her. She could now respond to his requests because she no longer felt that he was trying to control her. Her sense of significance and worth was returning because he was affirming her. She was feeling loved by him because he responded to her requests; thus, she was able to reciprocate his love.

Becky and David: "I admit I've had a lot of resentment toward you"

Becky's story is very similar. She applied the same principles and took basically the same steps that Jamal took. When she realized that David's behavior found its root in his need for significance and self-worth, and that his resentment of her was growing out of his need for love, she realized that her negative pattern had been compounding the problem. When she further realized that David's language of love was words of affirmation, she more deeply understood why he had withdrawn from her. She had given him exactly the opposite—complaining, condemning words. She understood more fully how her condemning words had pushed him to his social media and online games.

One night Becky apologized for her critical comments and asked his forgiveness. By admitting her imperfections, she was not blaming herself for every failure in their marriage. She also took responsibility for her own attitude and acknowledged how she had allowed her feelings of deep frustration to control her behavior. She determined not to let these emotions continue to control the way she related to David. Thus she had put into action principles one, four, and five of reality living.

"I have decided that I am going to focus on changing my negative behavior and try to make life nicer for you in the future. I am open to your suggestions as to how I can do this." And then Becky put the power of love to work and lauded David: "I am proud of your work. You've done a lot in your career. I admit I've been very critical of you because you have not done the things that I wanted. I realize that my criticism has hurt you. I focused on the negative rather than the positive."

David's response went something like this: "I never thought I would hear you say that. I thought I was the worst person in the world in your mind. I admit that I have had a lot of resentment toward you. I have not felt that you loved me for a long time and that you were trying to control my life. I was determined not to let that happen. I guess we both need to make some changes."

A week later, Becky asked for his suggestion on one thing she could do to make life easier for him. That first night, David did something that I have rarely seen happen—he said he would give her such a suggestion if she would also give him one. This set in motion a process that changed both of their lives.

When a marriage has been troubled for many years, such reciprocal openness is not the norm. But David was so impressed with the sincerity of Becky's approach that he reciprocated much more quickly than most.

Two years after Becky's new beginning, she was taking a coding class at the local community college. David painted the bedroom within six months, and when summer rolled around, he never missed a week at mowing the lawn. In Becky's words, "He became a totally different man. I can't believe we went so long in such misery and that things turned around so quickly."

Michelle and Dan: "I don't know how you've put up with me this long"

On the other hand, Michelle has not had such miraculous results, although she has seen positive change. Unlike Jamal and Becky, she was dealing with a different kind of irresponsibility. Her husband was basically irresponsible in all areas of life. He would not maintain a regular job, would not help her around the house, was not involved in parenting their two children, and essentially did only what he desired to do. For ten years, Michelle had carried the load financially and in all other areas of the marriage.

By the time I saw Michelle, Dan was suffering from deep depression. He was living out the message he had received from his alcoholic father that he was worthless and that he would never amount to anything. His anger at his father, exhibited toward fellow employees, remained a key reason he had never been able to hold a steady job. He did not feel loved by Michelle, and in his heart he felt that he did not deserve her love. He knew that he had failed her as a husband and often wondered why she put up with him.

All of these realities had to be considered in Michelle's approach at trying to be an agent of positive change in her desperate marriage. Remembering that Dan had responded well to her words of encouragement and affirmation in their dating relationship and in the first year of their marriage, and realizing that she had been giving him critical words for the last nine years, she decided to begin by acknowledging what she considered to be her major failure.

As hard as it was, this is what she said: "I've been thinking a lot about us, and I have realized that for the past several years, I have helped compound your problems by being critical of you. I know that my critical words have not helped you," she began. "I want you to know that I still love you even though I am sure that you haven't felt much love from me over the past few years.

"I must confess that I have been deeply disappointed with our marriage, and I do not wish to continue as we are. I know that a part of your problem is your depression, and I know that life has not been easy for you. I have decided that I will be willing to pay for your counseling if you would be willing to go. This is the only hope I see for your getting help and for our marriage getting better. If you are not willing to go for counseling, then I cannot remain in the marriage, even though I love you very much. If you are willing to go for counseling, I have a suggestion of a good counselor. He is one I can afford, and I think he will be able to help you. I want you to think about it and let me know your decision tomorrow."

Dan didn't say anything. So after a moment of silence, Michelle turned and walked out of the room. The next night, he was not there when she came home. He did not return in time for supper, which was not unusual. About 8:30 p.m. he came into the house, sat down on the couch, and stared at his phone, as was his habit. After Michelle got the kids to bed, she came in and said, "I can't tell you how much I love you, and I hope you know that I would not be doing what I am doing if I didn't really care about you and about us. I need to know your decision. Do you want to see a counselor or do you want to call our marriage quits?"

"I want to see a counselor," he said. "I know I've got problems, and I'm not getting any better. I don't know how you've put up with me this long."

"I'm glad," she said. "It's the only hope I see for either one of us." She reached for her purse and handed him the name of a counselor with a telephone number. "Here's the counselor I think you should see. Tomorrow, I want you to call and make an appointment. I've already checked. My insurance will pay for part of it, and I will take care of the rest until you get better and can get a job. Dan, I don't care how long it takes. I just want to see things different for you and for us."

The next day, Dan called the counselor, and the next week, he began the long process of dealing with his current depression, his long-term anger toward his father, and his learned patterns of irresponsibility. Within three months, he was looking for another job, and within three weeks, he found one. He continued his counseling for two years. The counselor was able to help him understand why he had lost his temper so often on the job, how he had transferred his anger at his father to fellow employees. Eventually, he learned how to let go of his anger toward his father. He found inner healing, and today he and his father have a cordial relationship.

More important, Dan learned how to process his anger on the job and at home. He and Michelle are in the process of building a meaningful marriage. They are still strapped with financial debt from the past, but for the first time, she believes that soon they will be able to deal with the debt. She has given Dan affirming words throughout the years of his recovery. He is slowly learning how to be a father to his children and how to express love to her on an emotional level. He acknowledges that it has been a long road, but he is encouraged by the progress he has seen. They both know that the journey is not over, but for the first time in ten years, they both believe that they are on a positive track.

Michelle's application of reality-living principles prompted her to act differently than either Jamal or Becky because the inner motivation of Dan's irresponsible behavior was vastly different from that of David and Suzanne. Still, she took responsibility for her own attitude in regard to Dan's irresponsibility and acknowledged her tendency to criticize him. Yet she did not label herself as a failure despite her imperfection. She understood that she could not change her husband, but she acted on the belief that she could influence him by encouraging him to seek counseling.

Finally, she continues to stand by Dan as he progresses, knowing that love is the most powerful weapon for good.

Remember: You can always take positive steps in a troubled marriage.

5

The
Workaholic
Spouse

When I opened the floor to questions in a marriage seminar, Andrea asked, "How do you live with a workaholic husband? My husband spends long hours at work and short hours at home. He leaves early in the morning and returns late at night. He sees his kids only when they are asleep. He sees me only when he is exhausted. His paycheck is his only contribution to the family."

By the time she had finished talking, numerous wives were nodding their heads, identifying with Andrea.

Who is this workaholic husband? (I am not suggesting that there are not workaholic wives, but this malady afflicts males far more frequently than females.) The workaholic husband is a man who has put all his marbles in the same bag. For him, his vocation is his life. He happens to be married and he happens, usually, to have children, but he is obsessed with his work. He doesn't understand why his wife is not happy with his accomplishments and all the material things that he provides for the family. But for the workaholic, his vocation is more than a search for daily bread—it is a search for daily meaning. His life has no balance.

Usually the workaholic enjoys his work. He bounces out of bed early in the morning with an eagerness to tackle the challenges of the day. When he comes home, he opens his laptop: more work, enough to keep him busy. Always busy but seldom satisfied. Enough is never enough. The sun shines bright on another opportunity, and he must seize it before dark.

He is often well respected in the community and in his professional circles, and he often receives accolades from his employer. On the other hand, his wife seldom views him as Mr. Wonderful. She is likely to be critical of him because he invests so little in their relationship and, if they have kids, is so uninvolved in their lives.

CONFESSIONS OF A WORKAHOLIC

Here is the story of a self-confessed workaholic. I first met Jim in Elgin, Illinois, at one of my marriage seminars. As I often do, I asked permission to record his story. Here are excerpts of what he said.

"I was like lots of men who have the idea of making it big, of becoming somebody. I started with the idea that if I worked harder and smarter, I would get ahead. I thought that if I worked long hours and applied my mind and came up with creative ideas, I would overcome the insecurities of my youth and would get ahead of my peers. I can't say that I really liked my work, but I was good at it. In a few years, I was moving up the ladder; I was reaching my goals, I was getting awards from my supervisor. But I must admit that I never felt a lot of satisfaction. I always thought I needed to do more.

"There were good times, of course. When I experienced the high of being salesman of the year, it felt good. I knew that everyone looked up to me. I knew that I had reached the goal that many of them were striving for. But when the euphoria of the moment was over, there was always that nagging feeling that I really should be much further ahead. When there were setbacks and I didn't do so well, I thought the only answer was to work harder.

"I spent long hours on the job. I hardly ever saw my kids awake. I would sneak into their bedrooms at night and look at their sleeping faces and tell myself that I was working hard to provide a good future for them. I was not there when they took their first steps, nor was I there when they first rode a bicycle. My nephew had the pleasure of launching them on wheels. At the time, I didn't realize that I was missing anything. I was thrilled when I found out on Sunday that my son had ridden a bicycle that week—'without training wheels,' as he said. I can hardly think about it without crying now, but then I was enthusiastic and told him how great that was. I guess in my own mind I thought he was taking the kind of steps that would one day get him where I was.

"The message I heard in my mind was, 'Go, go, go. Work, work, work.'"

"The message I heard in my mind was 'Go, go, go. Work, work, work.' I didn't have time to play with my kids and seldom had time to spend an evening making love to my wife. I had no friends except business acquaintances and certainly had no time for reading unless it related to my work.

"One Sunday afternoon my wife, Amy, got my attention with a proposed outing. She wouldn't say where we were going, only that she thought I'd like it. 'It won't take long, and you don't have to change clothes. Let's go.'

"I was only slightly interested but thought, *Here's an opportunity to do something she wants me to do. Maybe if I go with her, she will reciprocate with a little tenderness toward me tonight.* So Amy drove us to our destination.

"She drove me to the newest, nicest retirement center I have ever seen. The lawns were absolutely beautiful; the buildings were attractive—none of the drabness you expect at these places. We walked into the main building and saw a beautiful chandelier, a baby grand piano, and French provincial couches and chairs. Out back was a golf course. Amy started pointing out all of these amenities to me.

"I asked her, 'Why did you bring me out here? I'm only thirty-eight; we're not about to retire anytime soon.'

"She replied, 'But I wanted you to have a visual image of what it's going to be like, Jim, when you retire. With all the money you're making, you and I can afford to live in a place like this. We'll have a wonderful life together. You can play golf in the day, and we'll make love at night. We can attend movies and symphonies. We can have a real life, Jim, and all of this in only twenty-seven more years.'

"I said, 'Amy, you're out of your mind. What are you talking about? This is crazy.'

"She said, 'No, Jim. I'm very much in control of my mind, and I don't intend to wait twenty-seven years to have a real life with you. By that time, the children won't know you at all, and I'll be too old to have sex.' Her voice was firm; her words direct: 'I want you now, Jim, not in a retirement center. I'm tired of being a widow. I don't care if we ever live in a retirement center. I want to live now. I want us to have a life. I want the boys to be able to say their dad took them fishing. Then she said to me, 'I don't know what you want, Jim, but if all you want is to live in this beautiful retirement center, then you'll have to live here by yourself. This is not what I want. I want a real life with you—now. I'm not asking you to quit your job; I'm asking you to find a way to live before you retire.'"

Amy's words stunned her husband. "I don't remember crying since I was a child, but I cried that afternoon," Jim recalled. "Standing near the eighteenth green, my life flashed before me on the screen of my mind. I heard my father telling me that I would never amount to anything. I saw the years I had invested in trying to prove him wrong, and now I realized that I was in danger of losing everything that was important to me.

"I didn't blame Amy. I knew that she was telling me the truth. And through my tears I said, 'I'm sorry. I'm sorry. I know it's all been wrong. I was doing what I thought was important. But I was wrong.'

"That's what started a real change in my life. For a month, I analyzed what I could do about my all-consuming job. I concluded that I couldn't cut back my time there because of the pattern already in place, so I began searching for another job.

"It really was not that hard to leave when I found a new job. I've spent several years now rediscovering the real world. I've done a lot of thinking, looking back, and trying to learn why I had invested so many years thinking that material success was worth paying any cost to achieve."

Jim's conclusion? "I realize now that life is short, and we are very foolish if we do not keep a balance between work and family. I've observed that few people are ever satisfied with their success in their vocation no matter how much they have achieved. I'm convinced we never 'make it' because the goals keep expanding ahead of us. If in trying to be a success, you lose your wife and family, you've lost it all. I'll never regret the day that Amy forced me to face reality."

I must confess that by the time Jim finished his story, I had tears in my eyes, tears of joy to meet a man who had awakened from his stupor of obsession with work while his wife was still there and his boys still at home. I was eager to talk with Amy and find out the rest of the story. What motivated her? How did she come to her creative approach in getting Jim's attention? What had she experienced in the years before that? Later I'll tell you her side of the story, but first, let's take a look at what motivates men to be workaholics.

WHAT DRIVES THE WORKAHOLIC

What are the inner needs that drive the people we commonly call workaholics? Look again at the list.

Many workaholics suffer from a deep sense of inferiority. The seeds were probably planted in childhood. Parents (or others) relayed the message, "You're not as good as your brother. You're not as smart as your sister. You will never make it." As a child, the son or daughter internalized those messages; and as an adult, the messages still play in the mind of the workaholic. His work is an effort to overcome these feelings of inferiority. If he works hard enough and well enough, he will prove to himself and to others that he is not inferior. The person who overworks because he feels inferior must perform on a higher level than those around him. This often means that he must spend more hours away from home pursuing his goal of excellence.

This sense of inferiority often leads the workaholic to be a perfectionist. When he finishes a task, it seldom meets his own approval. I just don't think my superior will be happy with this, he reasons. So he spends another hour working on an already excellent report. This perfectionist tendency is another reason the workaholic rarely attacks problems around the house. He doesn't want to start a project because he doesn't believe that he can do it the way it ought to be done. Rather than proving himself a failure, he decides it is better not to begin.

Many workaholics also feel unloved. The message they received from their parents was not, "We love you," but rather, "We love you if . . . We love you if you make up your bed, put your dishes in the dishwasher, clean up your room, mow the grass, and make straight A's." Such conditional love sets a child up to become an adult workaholic.

Yes, workaholics are motivated by their need for love. And while they often receive accolades from their employers, which give them some sense of well-being, their often-distant relationships with their spouse and kids means they aren't feeling much love from the most significant people in their lives. Unless the workaholic awakens from his obsessive behavior as Jim did, he may live a lifetime with his need for love unmet.

Another need that motivates the workaholic is the need to achieve. The workaholic is often searching for significance. He believes that the fastest way to accomplish something of lasting value is to pursue his vocation with a passion, to amass a successful financial portfolio, own a nice house with expensive furnishings. He is searching for significance in the wrong places, but he has not yet made that discovery.

HIDING FROM YOUR SPOUSE

Some workaholics are also hiding from their spouses. They use busyness to avoid getting in touch with their own feelings and/or the feelings of their spouses. For some people, it is much easier

For some people, it is much easier to work than it is to relate to a spouse on an emotional level.

to work than it is to relate to a spouse on an emotional level. Someone has said, "Men love competition but hate confrontation." Such men see confrontation with their wives as a lose/lose proposition.

A husband doesn't want his wife to lose in a confrontation because she will treat him with even greater harshness, or she will withdraw. He certainly doesn't want to lose the confrontation because this confirms the parental message of his incompetence. Thus, he stays at the office to avoid coming home to a wife who makes him feel incompetent as a husband or father. For the workaholic, the thought of facing a discontented wife is enough to keep him away until she is asleep. If he views himself as incompetent, the last thing he wants is for his wife to concur. If by virtue of his hard work he has been able to convince himself that he is a success, he certainly does not want to hear his wife rebuff him and repeat the message of his parents. If the criticism from his wife has been constant and long-term, he may conclude that he will never please her; thus, he invests his energy in his vocation where he has some measure of success and recognition.

Of course, working wives can become workaholics, too. Often they stay at work, either at the office or in the home study, in order to hide from their husbands and avoid a confrontation. Some women also become workaholics to escape a spouse's condemnation; they choose to work long hours away from their husbands. When it comes to working to avoid condemnation, even religious service can become an escape. Ministers often fall into this category. Their obsession becomes serving God. Their view of God as a holy creature who demands perfection or at least demands that their good deeds outweigh the bad deeds keeps them diligently working to please Him. Ironically, this is the opposite of the true Christian message; yet many ministers and parishioners read the Bible through the grid of parental condemnation and perfectionistic expectations. Thus, they work hard in the service of God.

One minister's wife said to me, "My husband preaches against adultery but, in fact, he is committing adultery. I don't mean he is having an affair with a woman; I mean the church has become his mistress. I am his housekeeper, and our children are orphans. Everyone praises him for being such a wonderful pastor. He is 'always available.' I'm sorry, but I don't share the view of the congregation. I can't believe that it pleases God for him to give his family so little attention while he ministers to others."

I listened and helped the wife decide on an action that would catch the ears and heart of her husband. She urged her husband to attend a national men's conference. Her husband listened as an African-American football player talked about the importance of the male's role in the African-American family. Like a bolt of lightning, God's voice struck the pastor's heart in regard to his failure in his own family. Later, when the speaker asked that each man turn to another man and "confess their faults one to another," this pastor turned to his fellow pastor and confessed that he had failed his wife and children. That was the beginning of a radical change in his ministry—and his marriage.

AMY'S SIDE OF THE STORY

Of course, the workaholic is a very responsible person—that may even be part of the initial attraction to his or her mate. For instance, Amy described her earlier years with Jim, before their dramatic confrontation on the lawn of the retirement center.

"Jim was twenty-four when we got married, and I was twenty-three. I was so in love with him. He was my ideal of a successful man. He had already accomplished a lot since finishing college, and I knew that we would have a wonderful life together. During courtship, he was everything I had dreamed of—kind, courteous, thoughtful, attentive, and, yes, good-looking. I knew he would be a perfect husband.

"The first two years of our marriage were exciting. We were buying a house, getting the furniture, getting settled in. But then Jim got a promotion. From that point on, it seemed like everything changed. We had more money but saw less of each other.

"I didn't like what was happening with his time, and I told Jim that I felt like his job was more important than I was. He assured me that it wouldn't be like this forever but that the next two or three years were going to require a lot of his time. I understood that and I was willing to sacrifice if it were temporary.

"In a year or so, the baby came, and my life was absorbed with caring for him. Jim's mother and my mother gave me a lot of help the first year. Actually, I think their help maintained my stability. They often baby-sat while I got away for some relaxation. I even met Jim for lunch a few times. Those were special times. But then his parents moved out of town, and my mother got sick. I really needed Jim, but he was not there for me. Three years had passed, but things were worse than ever.

"When I talked to Jim about it, he said that I didn't appreciate his hard work: 'You should be thankful for all that I provide for you and the baby,' he told me.

"I was thankful, but I didn't feel that we were living a normal life. I felt that Jim was obsessed with his work and that I certainly was not at the top of his list of priorities."

For the next several years Amy alternated between an aggressive and a passive approach. "Part of the time, I would give Jim angry lectures and accuse him of not loving me. I even accused him once of having an affair. I told him that he would live to regret the day he got that job. I complained about the job; I criticized his superiors. I told him about my lack of respect for the management of a company that would require a man to spend so much time at work. Then I would go for long periods of time saying nothing, but suffering and showing by my behavior that I was unhappy with Jim and our relationship. During these times, we had fewer arguments, but the pain was more intense for me. I steadily grew to a place of hopelessness. I really had come to believe that Jim really didn't care."

TOUGH, FIRM, KIND

Change came when Amy read a book about inner motives behind people's behavior.

"I began to realize that Jim's behavior had little to do with me and far more to do with him. I remembered the stories he had told me when we were dating, of how his father criticized his schoolwork and his athletic efforts. I remembered specific stories about his father, such as the Saturday Jim mowed the lawn, and his father came out and pointed out a spot he had missed.

"His father was seldom complimentary and almost always critical. There was no question about it; he had gotten the message as a child that he was not good enough and that his father was not pleased with him.

"For the first time, I realized that much of Jim's motivation for working so much was to prove to his father that he 'could make it.' He was trying to prove his own self-worth, and I realized that his plan was working. His accomplishments on the job were giving him the affirmation he needed from others, and I really believed that Jim was feeling good about his accomplishments. The problem, of course, was that I was feeling left out."

Amy also realized that her critical attitude was much like that of Jim's father and that she was driving him away by her critical comments about his work. So she decided to stop making critical comments and start giving Jim positive comments about his job.

"I started telling him the good things I heard people say about his company. I started saying things like, 'Your supervisor must be very proud of you. You must have saved the company thousands of dollars with that decision.' I started expressing appreciation for the way he provided for me and the children. I started giving him the affirmation that I knew he needed.

"Over a period of a couple of months, the atmosphere between the two of us began to improve. We weren't having fights, and Jim seemed to enjoy the few times we went out to dinner. But his work patterns did not change. I felt that I had changed my attitude, and I had stopped my negative behavior and had started giving positive affirmation. But it didn't seem to be influencing Jim to make any changes."

So what made Amy think of the visit to the retirement center? A friend of hers suggested Amy try using "tough love," saying that love sometimes must be hard and firm and that if we really care about someone, we will confront the person in a kind but firm way. "I thought about it for a long time, and I realized that Jim was a good man but that unless he was shocked, his obsession with work was not going to change.

"So I thought about a creative way that I could break the news to him that I was very unhappy with our relationship and unwilling to continue in the present mode. I felt that over the past couple of months, I had demonstrated my soft love for him by changing my behavior. Now it was time for tough love.

"What I said to him at the retirement center was a speech I had rehearsed many times. I said it with emotion, I said it with sincerity, and I said it with firmness. Thank God, he listened."

Later Jim agreed to go with Amy for marriage counseling. And the counselor helped him make the decision to find another vocation that would

Resolve not to let your negative attitude turn into negative actions.

demand less of his time and would give him the freedom to start over with a more balanced perspective on life. Amy calls that and other changes Jim made "pretty radical" but very helpful to their marriage.

With a twinkle in her eye, she told me, "I am actually looking forward to living with Jim at the retirement center. I'm just glad I don't have to wait till then to start living."

Jim said, "I'm not sure we can afford to live at that retirement center. It doesn't matter. Wherever we are, we are going to enjoy our relationship."

I believe that Amy's efforts at soft and tender love were important before she came to her tough-love approach. Jim might not have had the same response on the eighteenth green of the retirement center golf course if she had not recognized his inner need for significance and self-worth, understood the role of his father's condemning messages in motivating him to become a workaholic, and stopped her critical remarks about his work, replacing them with affirming words. I believe that tough love must always be preceded by tender love.

Remember that love is looking out for the other person's interest. The first step is trying to understand the behavior of your spouse, the inner motivations that drive him or her, and then asking yourself whether your past responses to that negative behavior have actually made the problem worse. Most of the time, the first step in becoming an agent of positive change in a desperate marriage is to change your own attitude based on a better understanding of your spouse's behavior.

Also remember that reality living encourages you to take responsibility for your own attitude toward your spouse. If your spouse is a workaholic, be honest with yourself about your attitude toward his or her behavior. But then resolve not to let your negative attitude turn into negative actions. Instead, follow Amy's example and seek to be an agent of positive change, admitting your imperfections and realizing that you cannot change your spouse, but you most certainly can influence him or her.

When you change your thinking and your negative responses, you become free to take a new approach. You open the way for love to do its powerful work.

6

The Depressed Spouse

Joe should have been happy. After being downsized out of his job several years ago, he had launched a new business and was finally seeing the fruit of his hard work pay off. But sitting in my office, he had other things on his mind. "It's my wife, Dr. Chapman. She seems so unhappy. I don't remember the last time I saw her smile. She's so negative, always gloom and doom about the business and everything else. It isn't like her."

He went on to share that his wife, Kara, normally high-energy, had no ambition and rarely ate with him and the kids. "She must have lost forty pounds over the last year. She's up and down all night long; says she can't sleep. This, of course, makes it hard for me to sleep. She worries about everything.

"To be truthful, life is pretty miserable at our house. I feel sorry for the kids, although they get more attention than I do.

But I know that they must wonder what is wrong with their mother. She seems so depressed all the time."

With that brief description, Joe had just described the common symptoms of depression. For the depressed person, the mood will be sad, the thinking negative, and the behavior lifeless. Physically, the depressed person may exhibit loss of appetite and loss of weight, sleep too much or too little, lose their sexual drive. These characteristics are often accompanied by general anxiety. The person will express fears, uncertainty, and indecisiveness.

Thousands of men and women can identify with Joe's frustration because they too live with a depressed spouse. Unfortunately, many of them have little understanding of the causes and cures of depression. They simply do not understand why their spouses cannot "snap out of it and get on with life." Lack of understanding often begets frustration and a critical spirit. A spouse's critical words actually compound the problem.

WHY ARE THEY DEPRESSED?

Understanding depression is not a simple matter. There are many types of depression, each with its own specific cause and each producing varying levels of depressed feelings and energy. It is beyond the scope of this chapter to give a full treatise on understanding depression, but let me give a brief overview. It is helpful to think of three categories of depression.

First, depression may be the by-product of a physical illness. For example, when you have a full-blown case of influenza, you don't care what is going on at the office. You want to lie still and sleep as much as possible. You lose all interest in the outside world. You temporarily check out; your mind and emotions have moved into a depressed state. It is nature's way of protecting you from constant anxiety about what you are missing in the real world.

Fortunately, the influenza passes, and your depressive mood lifts, although you may have noted that it tends to hang on for a day or two after your physical symptoms are gone. It often takes the mind a couple of days to get back to its normal state. More serious illnesses can lead to deeper and more lasting depression.

A second kind of depression is often called *situational depression* or *reactive depression*. This type of depression grows out of a particularly painful situation in life. Most of these experiences involve a sense of loss. For example, depression often follows the loss of a spouse by death or divorce, the loss of a job, the loss of a child to college, the loss of parents to death, the loss of a friendship, the loss of money, the loss of health. Depression may also arise over the loss of a dream, such as a happy, fulfilling marriage, the loss of the love feelings that you once had for your spouse, or the loss of hope that your marriage will ever be as fulfilling as you once hoped.

A third category of depression is rooted in some biochemical disorder, which has put the mind and emotions in a state of disequilibrium. Sometimes this is referred to as *endogenous depression*. The word *endogenous* means "from within the body," and the biological-chemical change inside the body is its source. This depression is a physical disease.

There are various forms of biological depression. Some are related directly to the brain where something goes wrong with the electrical and neurochemical transmissions. Others are related to disorders of the endocrine system. The glands of the endocrine system (thyroid, parathyroid, thymus, pancreas, pituitary, adrenal, ovaries, and gonads) produce hormones that are released into the bloodstream to perform various functions. Lowered or heightened levels of these hormones can produce depression. Also, certain disorders of metabolism can produce depression. The body is constantly assimilating food, breaking it into substances that can be stored and used as energy. When things go wrong in the metabolic system, depression can sometimes result. For example, abnormally low blood sugar levels can produce feelings of emotional instability and depression.

There may well be biological reasons why females are more prone to depression than males. The female reproductive organs are known to create mood swings. Premenstrual syndrome, commonly known as PMS, is the depression at the onset of menstruation; it is a common occurrence. Doctors now also recognize that some women suffer from premenstrual dysphoric disorder (PMDD), a more severe, sometimes disabling form of premenstrual syndrome.[1] Women in menopause often face bouts of depression. The variation in estrogen levels markedly influences the mood of women.

Fifteen percent of women experience "significant depression" after giving birth, and the numbers are higher for teenage mothers, women dealing with poverty, a history of PMDD, or an infant in the neonatal intensive care unit (NICU). Symptoms of postpartum depression include:

- Feelings of anger or irritability
- Lack of interest in the baby
- Appetite and sleep disturbance
- Crying and sadness
- Feelings of guilt, shame or hopelessness
- Loss of interest, joy or pleasure in things you used to enjoy
- Possible thoughts of harming the baby or yourself[2]

The good news about biologically caused depression is that it is readily treated with medication. The bad news is that only about one-third of all depressions are biological depressions. The far more common depression is situational depression. Medications are of little or no value in treating situational depression unless, of course, the situational depression has gone on for a long period of time and has affected the biochemistry of the body. It is true that extended periods of depression, whatever the original cause, may lead to problems in the neurochemical transmission system in the brain. Thus, medication may be a part of a treatment program.

Nearly all of us, from time to time, experience brief bouts of situational depression. These are simply our normal responses to the problems of everyday life. Usually we are not overwhelmed by these feelings of depression, nor do we allow them to control our behavior, and in a few days these feelings have passed; the depression was of little consequence in the overall flow of life.

> *If the clinically depressed person does not begin treatment, the depression will tend to deepen.*

At other times, however, depression becomes a serious problem. The term often used for these more serious periods of depression is *clinical depression*. This term is used in many ways, but most commonly it is used to refer to a depression that has lingered for many weeks—or perhaps months—and that has affected the normal functions of life, such as sleep, appetite, capacity for work, and social relationships. As a clinical depression, the condition needs treatment; it is not likely to go away simply with more time. If the clinically depressed person does not begin treatment, the depression will tend to deepen, and the person will become more and more withdrawn from the realities of life. It is the task of the treatment specialist to determine the cause of the depression and to suggest a course of treatment.[3]

THE DOCTOR'S ROLE, THE COUNSELOR'S ROLE

Most depressed persons who reach out for help turn first to their medical doctor. However, most medical doctors do not have time to give a thorough analysis to determine the cause of the depression. Thus, physicians often prescribe what is commonly referred to as an antidepressant medication. If the depression happens to have a biological cause, then the medication can be helpful. It usually takes three to four weeks to determine if a given medication is producing positive results. If it does not produce such results, the physician often will try another type of medication. It is not uncommon for a doctor to prescribe three or four different types of medication before there is any noticeable change in the patient's depressive state.

However, if the individual's depression does not have a biological cause, the medication will be of little value. Since only about a third of depression has a biological root, it is far more advisable for the depressed person to begin with a trained therapist who has experience in treating those who are depressed. By nature of his or her profession, the therapist has more time to explore the root cause of the depression. If it is in fact a situational depression, then counseling is the best method of treatment. The person must come to process his or her grief over the loss that stimulated the depression or learn to adapt to the situation that caused the depression. This is best done over a period of time with a trained therapist. If the counselor discerns that there may be a biochemical aspect to the person's depression, the counselor normally will refer the individual to a psychiatrist, who, after evaluation, will recommend a particular medication. A combination of medication and counseling is the best treatment for these individuals.

As for depressions that are the byproduct of a physical disease such as influenza, cancer, or any other chronic disease, counseling can be helpful for the depression while medical treatment is certainly recommended to treat the disease itself. Usually, there is mutual respect for the value of both the physician and the counselor, each dealing with a different aspect of an individual's problem.

In all depressions, the spiritual aspect of life is an important part of the patient's treatment. Most professionals recognize a connection between the physical, psychological, and spiritual aspects of life. The counselor who is unwilling to explore the area of spiritual renewal is, in my opinion, overlooking one of the most helpful aspects of treating depression. On the other hand, there is always the danger of religious enthusiasts who see all depression as a spiritual problem and thus heap more guilt on the depressed person. Such an approach, far from being helpful, actually exacerbates the depression. The healthiest road of treatment involves an honest and in-depth evaluation of all three elements: physical, psychological, and spiritual. Depression is not an incurable disease. Even those who have been depressed for months or sometimes years can find relief with the proper treatment.

JOE: WHAT NOW?

As Joe sat sharing his struggle with his wife's behavior, it was obvious to me that he had little understanding of these concepts. He knew that Kara had a problem, and he knew that her problem was causing him great frustration. But he wasn't even sure what her problem was, and he certainly had no idea of how to help her. For a while he had tried to listen to her sympathetically. He had given her his best advice. But he had seen no progress and became frustrated. Eventually he started saying things like, "You're destroying our marriage and hurting the kids. You need to get hold of yourself."

Joe arrived at my office in one final, last-ditch effort. He had been thinking of divorce for some time, feeling that he could not live the rest of his life in such a stressful marriage.

I was sympathetic with Joe's frustration, but I knew in my heart that divorce was not the answer. My first suggestion was to ask him to read a book on depression. Until he gained some understanding of the nature of depression, I knew that he would not be able to be an agent of positive change in his marriage. When he came back the following week, he had read the entire book and said to me, "There is no question about it. Kara is depressed. She has all the characteristics. I don't know if it is a biological depression or a situational depression, but I know that she is depressed." I could tell that he had read the book thoughtfully.

Now that Joe and I had both had agreed that Kara struggled with depression, the question was how to get her the help she needed. I asked, "Do you think that she would come in to see me if you told her that you have talked with me about your own frustrations in the marriage and that I had requested that she make an appointment?"

"I don't know," Joe responded. "She hasn't been out of the house in at least two weeks."

I suggested to Joe that he try to have Kara call my office, and if I didn't hear from her within a week, I would reach out to her. Joe agreed, and I added, "One other request. Don't mention the word *depression* to your wife. Just tell her that you talked with me about your frustrations in the marriage." (I didn't want her to get the idea that the two of us had ganged up, diagnosed her problem, and were now out to cure her.)

AN INTERVIEW WITH KARA

The next week came and went without a call from Kara. The following week, I left a voice mail and asked that she come in to see me. Four days later, she was in my office, with her clothes hanging loosely on her thin body and her face void of expression. I told her that after hearing from Joe about his struggles, I wanted to hear her perspective on her marriage. "And I want you to be honest with me," I said.

I asked the normal questions regarding how long she had been married, how many children she had, and, on a scale of 0–10, to tell me how healthy she viewed her marriage. Her answer to the last question was "2." At least she was in touch with that reality.

When I asked if her marriage had always been this unhappy, her response was no—until her mother died. "She was sick a long time, and it was really a hard thing to go through. Then she died, and somehow I just . . . lost my spark. Nothing seemed to matter anymore, including Joe and the kids, although I was able to at least kind of go through the motions with the children.

"At first I felt sorry for Joe because I knew I was not being a wife to him. But then after his angry words, I figured he didn't deserve a wife, and I cared even less. Nothing matters anymore. I really wish I could die. It would be better for me and my family."

"How would you describe your feelings?" I continued.

"I have no energy," she said. "I have no interest in anything. I just try to sleep as much as I can."

"Do you feel angry toward Joe?" I inquired.

"No. I don't feel anything toward him," she said.

"Have you ever talked with your medical doctor about your feelings and your lack of energy?" I inquired.

"Right after Mom died, I went to see him once. He told me that I was depressed, and he gave me some antidepressants. I took two or three of them, and they made me dizzy, so I didn't take them anymore."

"Have you ever known anyone who suffered from depression?" I asked.

"Not really," she said. "My mother told me about my grand-mother and said that she died from depression after her son, my mother's brother, was killed in a car accident. But I never knew my grandmother."

"I've known lots of people who have suffered from depression," I said. "And none of them died from it. In fact, they are no longer suffering from depression. They are living happy lives." I went on to give Kara a summary of depression, its symptoms, its causes and its cures. I asked her if she thought she was depressed.

"I know I am depressed," she said. "I just don't know what to do about it. I'm not sure I can do anything about it."

"Sometimes when we have been depressed for a long time," I said, "we get the feeling of hopelessness, and we think that we will never get better. But I want you to know that depression can be healed. It takes some time, but when it is all over, you can be happy again. You and Joe could have a good life together, and you could be the mother you always wanted to be.

"I have a good friend who specializes in helping people over-come depression. If I could set up an appointment with her, would you be willing to meet with her for a few weeks and let her help you walk through the valley of your depression and walk out to the mountain on the other side, where the sun is shining and the flowers are blooming?"

"I don't know if I have the energy, Dr. Chapman."

"I understand," I said. "But would you be willing to try?"

"I guess so," she said. (Most people who are deeply depressed are not highly motivated to enter counseling. Acquiescence is about as much as you can expect.)

"All right," I said. "I will set up an appointment for you and have her office call you. After you have met with her six times, I want to see you again and find out how you are doing." Kara agreed, and she left my office as slowly as she had entered.

DOS AND DON'TS FOR JOE

The next week I saw Joe and recounted my time with Kara and the strategy I had suggested to get her on the path to treatment. I asked him to be as positive as he could with her, and I gave him the following list of "dos and don'ts" in his efforts to help her. If you or someone you know is married to a depressed husband or wife, I recommend this same list to you.

Don'ts

1. Don't tell her that she has nothing to be depressed about.
2. Don't tell her that everything is going to be okay.
3. Don't tell her to "snap out of it" or "pull yourself together."
4. Don't tell her that the problem is a spiritual problem.
5. Don't tell her that the problem stems from her family.
6. Don't tell her why you think she is depressed.
7. Don't give advice; rather, encourage her to listen to her counselor.

Dos

1. Do tell her that you are glad she is going for counseling.
2. Do let her know that if she wants to talk, you want to listen.
3. Do receive her feelings without condemning them. If she says, "I'm feeling empty," your response might be, "Would you like to tell me about it?"
4. Do continue to take care of the children and things around the house.
5. Do look for life-threatening symptoms (suicidal talk or actions).
6. Do inform her counselor of such talk.

7. Do tell her that you believe in her and that you know she will come out of this.

8. Do encourage her to make decisions, but don't force her.

"Remember, you can encourage her, you can be supportive, you can create a climate for her healing," I told Joe. I reminded him of the third reality-living principle: I cannot change others, but I can influence them.

"Just remind yourself, however, that you cannot be Kara's therapist." Joe could allow his love for Kara to do its powerful work for good, but I also knew that she needed the skilled guidance of a therapist.

I reminded him that, despite his frustrations, he could be an agent of positive change in his desperate marriage. I encouraged him to recognize his attitude toward his wife's depression. And then I reminded him that his attitude was *his* responsibility, not his wife's. Even though Kara was depressed, Joe did not have to sink into those feelings as well. He could choose to remain positive, despite the negative situation.

> *Even though Kara was depressed, Joe did not have to sink into those feelings as well.*

I knew this would not be easy. I also encouraged him to admit to Kara his imperfections in the way he had responded to her depression. He began to understand that his anger and frustration had only deepened her problem. He also began to understand that his imperfections did not mean he was a complete failure.

I agreed to see Joe periodically while Kara was in counseling, and we agreed that when her therapist recommended, I would begin marriage counseling with them.

When I saw Kara after her first six appointments with the counselor, there was a noticeable difference. She sat up straighter in the chair, she looked at me more frequently. Her face was not as forlorn, and she had gained a few pounds.

Her major question for me was, "What about taking medication?" The counselor had asked that she see a psychiatrist for an evaluation and perhaps take some medication. Kara was reluctant to do this. I encouraged her to follow the advice of her counselor. I assured her that the counselor had worked with many other depressed people and that if she thought there might be a biological aspect to her depression, it was worth checking out. I reminded her that if the depression did have some biological basis, that medication could be extremely helpful. (I assured her that antidepressants are not addictive and that taking the medication was not a sign of weakness but of wisdom.)

With Kara's permission, her counselor shared with me that although her depression seemed to be brought on by her mother's death, it was really rooted in the fact that her father had sexually abused her as a child. Her mother's death had brought all these feelings to the surface, and these plunged her into depression. The depression went untreated for almost a year and affected her physiologically. Thus at that point, the medication was a necessary part of the treatment process.

Eight months later, when I began to do marriage counseling with Joe and Kara, it was obvious to me at this juncture that she had made tremendous progress. She was smiling, even joking at times. She was no longer spending her days in bed but was jogging, cooking, taking the kids shopping, and singing with her church worship team from time to time. She and Joe were working toward regular date nights.

After approximately six to seven months of marriage counseling, I released them. Today they have a healthy marriage, are actively involved with their extended family, have become leaders in the church, and are currently attending a class to develop their parenting skills.

Joe and Kara's case illustrates that the causes of depression are not always readily discerned. It also shows that most of us can handle the normal depression that lasts for a day or a week, but when depression persists and begins to affect your daily behavior, it is time to reach out for treatment.

GRIEVING A LOSS

At the heart of any treatment program for situational depression is helping the person walk through the grief process. Almost always, situational depression centers on the loss of something, whether it be job, parent, child, integrity, health, marriage, or the loss of a dream. If the person is not allowed to grieve over the loss, he or she will almost always end up depressed.

Sonya's husband, William, went into a depression almost immediately after his father's death. Fortunately, Sonya recognized the symptoms and realized that depression often follows a significant loss. She also realized that the process of grieving is facilitated by talking about the loss. So she started asking William questions about his father, William Senior—more questions than she had ever asked in her life—and he started talking.

She learned of William's positive memories of helping his dad around the family farm when he was growing up. She also learned of painful memories that he had of his father's harsh discipline. She continued to ask questions, and he continued to talk. She knew that she was helping him work through his grief and walk out of depression.

At first William was reluctant to talk about his father. He made such comments as, "He's gone. There's no need to talk about him." But Sonya would not be brushed off. She knew that he needed to talk, and she wanted to listen. She realized that his loss was not simply the death of his father, but that his father's death had touched varied pain from his childhood—memories of basketball games where his dad was not in the stands to cheer; memories of his father's harsh words, but no memory of his father saying the words, "I love you."

Seriously depressed people will seldom take initiative to help themselves.

William had never shared these thoughts and feelings with anyone, but Sonya had the wisdom to pull them out and to listen sympathetically without trying to heal the wounds herself. She said such things as, "I can see how that would have been painful; how did you handle it at the time?" She stayed away from condemning statements, such as, "That was such a little thing—why did that bother you?" She listened and affirmed. She let him grieve. She helped him grieve.

She realized that she could not change his feelings of sorrow but that she could influence him toward healing by getting him to talk. Although Sonya was sometimes frustrated with William's distance and lack of communication, she chose not to let those emotions control her actions. Instead, she chose to be an agent of positive change in her marriage and take positive action. She let her love for William become a powerful weapon for his healing.

In the first six months after William's father died, they had several of these conversations. Then every three months, she would bring up his dad again. For two years, she followed this process. At the end of two years, William's grief work was done, and he was able to move on with life. He never entered a deep depression because he was allowed to grieve his losses. However, if his wife had not been there, there is the strong possibility that William would have gone into a deep and long depression after his father's death. That could have required extensive therapy for healing. Helping people grieve by talking about their losses is preventive medicine. It often averts a serious depression.

The wise spouse will make time to gain information on depression and grief. Sooner or later, we will all experience losses in life. These losses can lead us to healthy grief or unhealthy depression. The spouse who understands depression and the process of grief can be extremely helpful in these times of crisis.[4] The spouse who does not understand the process can actually compound the suffering of his or her mate. Numerous resources on the subject of depression are available on the internet, in any public library, and through your pastor or a therapist of your acquaintance. The wise spouse will be informed and ready to help facilitate the process of grief and to ward off depression.

REMEMBER WHAT *YOU* CAN DO

Let me summarize some of the key elements in helping a depressed spouse. Seriously depressed people will seldom take initiative to help themselves. They are overwhelmed with the darkness of life. Their constant companion is a sense of helplessness. Therefore, be a caring spouse, showing compassion and being encouraging.

The role of the caring spouse is extremely important. If your spouse's depression lingers more than a few weeks, encourage him or her to talk with a counselor, pastor, or a physician. If such encouragement goes unheeded, then tell your spouse that you are going for help because you cannot sit idly by and watch him or her suffer.

Remember to apply reality-living principles, especially principles three and six: I cannot change others, but I can influence others. Love is the most powerful weapon for good in the world.

My suggestion is that you contact a counselor or pastor and express your concern about your spouse and how his or her depression is affecting you. Ask the counselor for recommended readings and advice on how you can be helpful to your spouse. Learn everything you can about depression. Review the "dos and don'ts" listed earlier in this chapter.

Be sure to dismiss the myths. There is hope for your depressed spouse and for your marriage.

Hopefully, your efforts to be an agent of positive change in your marriage will serve to motivate your spouse to reach out for professional help.

Whatever the source of depression, there is always hope if the depressed person can get appropriate physical, psychological, or spiritual help.

FOR FURTHER HELP

- NAMI.org
- postpartum.net

PART 3

Abusive
Spouses

The Controlling Spouse

J odie felt like a "hamster in a cage."

She was a longtime acquaintance, but I hadn't seen her for years. I was thrilled to see her at one of my marriage seminars near St. Louis. We were catching up with each other when my thrill turned to sadness. Jodie recounted the pain of her twenty-seven-year marriage to Roger, a man who had been successful in his career but a failure in his marriage. Jodie had dreamed of a partnership where she and Roger could share thoughts, feelings, desires, and work together as a team in facing life. Roger, on the other hand, was an obsessive controller. He had no concept of teamwork. His father was extremely domineering, and he was repeating the model of his father.

Jodie explained, "Every time I come home, he wants to know where I've been and what I've done . . . He has to have the final decision in everything. Our social life is almost nil because he never wants to do anything with anyone else. He's told our children that he will not pay for their college unless they go to the university of his choice. Gary, I feel like I am a bird in a cage. No, a hamster in a cage—I don't have wings anymore."

In further conversation, I found out that Jodie had been suffering from anxiety attacks for the past two or three years. She described these attacks in the following way: "I get short of breath and my chest gets tight. I feel like I'm suffocating. They come on with no warning and leave me helpless." The anxiety attacks had led her to seek counseling. The counselor suggested that the attacks might be directly related to the stress she was living with in her marriage. Jodie didn't want to admit it, but she knew the counselor was correct. The counselor referred her to a physician for medication, but she and the counselor knew that this was not the long-term answer to her problem. Something had to change in her miserable marriage.

She had dreamed of a partnership where she and her husband could work together as a team in facing life.

JUST LIKE MOM OR DAD

Who are these controlling men (and women) who seek to dominate their spouses?[1] Many times they are some of the most respected people in the community, and often they are unaware of their controlling behavior. They are simply following a lifestyle that to them seems normal. They are either living out the model that they observed in childhood, or they are following the script written in their personality. Let's look at each of these.

Roger, Jodie's husband, fell into the first category. His father was an authoritarian role model. He made the money, and he ran the house. The only decisions his wife made were how to dress the kids and what the family would eat. Even in these areas, he sometimes criticized her. All other decisions Roger's father made himself. He prided himself on being a successful man and ruling his family well. His children and his wife were respected in the community. The whole family was active in the local church, and Roger's dad often related his controlling behavior to the biblical mandate that "the husband is the head of the wife." His father exuded self-confidence and was known as a man who made things happen.

Roger's mother, in the early days of her marriage, had complained about her husband's controlling behavior, but that was before Roger was born. After the children came, she busied herself with them and accepted her lot in life. She was pleased that her husband was a good provider, and she never questioned any of his decisions. If she disagreed, she kept her thoughts to herself, and in due time her pained emotions subsided. She did not have an intimate emotional relationship with Roger's dad, but she assumed that her marriage was pretty much like that of all the women she knew.

Roger was simply following the model with which he had grown up. He was a good provider, so he wondered why Jodie was complaining. Why was she not willing to play her role as well as he was playing his?

If she had confronted him, he never would have admitted that his behavior was controlling. He could not understand why Jodie would have felt anything but gratitude. She could not ask for a better husband than he.

Unfortunately, Roger never changed. Two years later, I got a note from Jodie telling me that she and Roger were divorced and that she had married a "wonderful" man.

BORN TO DOMINATE

There is another kind of individual who is not likely to recognize his or her controlling patterns. This is the person who has what psychologists often call a dominating or controlling personality. This person is not following the model of parents; he is playing out the script that is written in his personality.

These are people who often become leaders in the community, on the job, or in the church. They are the kind of people who take authority, solve problems, make decisions, and get things done. They are movers and shakers. Usually they have a high level of self-confidence and believe they can accomplish anything. Give them a task, and it will be done. They produce results; however, dominating persons are not in touch with emotions—their own or other people's. Their attitude is, "What difference does it make how you feel? Let's get on with the job."

Dominant personalities are goal-oriented, not relationship-oriented. They get things done, but they often hurt people in the process. To them, that is simply part of the cost of reaching the objective. The dominant personality is always ready to argue and convince an opponent that he or she is wrong. The dominant person sometimes uses intimidation—whatever is necessary to reach the goal.

These types of people are often rigid in their orientation. Their attitude is, "There is only one thing to do—finish the task. There is only one way to do it—my way; and there is only one time to do it—now." Once they have accepted a task, they do not want to be bothered with such questions as, "Why are we doing this?" And once they have a plan in action, they don't want to be slowed with annoying questions. such as, "Is this the best way to do it?"

When the person with a dominating personality marries, he or she brings that personality into the marriage and does what comes naturally. Getting married itself was a task for this individual. Before the wedding, the dominating personality did whatever was necessary to reach the goal; after the wedding, the task was accomplished. Now it is time for another task. Thus, there is often drastic behavior change in this person after marriage. Many wives testify that once the wedding day was past, the man they married vanished forever.

Many wives testify that once the wedding day was past, the man they married vanished forever.

In the marriage, the dominating personality will make decisions quickly, often not involving the spouse in the decision at all. "Why bother him? I can get this done. Let him spend his energies somewhere else" is the attitude. If the spouse confronts the dominating partner about not being involved in the decisions, the partner is amazed it is an issue. "It's something I could handle. Why would you want to waste your time talking about it?" In the dominating person's mind, he is not controlling but being "efficient."

PHILLIP, THE EFFICIENCY EXPERT

Phillip was a dominating personality. Early in life, he decided that he wanted to retire at fifty. He was an engineer with a good job, on a fast track toward promotion. He felt good about his accomplishments on the job, and he also applied his skills in managing finances at home. He put himself and his wife, Gina, on a strict budget. In his mind, he was allowing plenty for food, clothing, maintenance, and so on. He included a monthly amount for recreation and even some "spending money" for himself and Gina. He covered all the bases, and the budget was extremely efficient.

The problem was that Gina did not agree with the budget. Phillip saw her objections as a threat to his leadership and an affront to his skills. He was willing to explain the budget to her one time, but when she still did not agree, he became angry and withdrew. He knew his plan was workable; why was she making such a fuss? Eventually, Gina stopped talking about it, and he took her silence as acquiescence. So he moved on to apply his efficient planning to other areas of money management.

He analyzed the household to determine how to get the most efficiency out of all the appliances. He put water-saver shower-heads on all the showers. He made improvements on the windows in order to get the best rate from the electric company. He installed efficiency filters on the furnace. Later, he got a wood-stove, which in his mind would save a large amount on heating cost. That was when Gina exploded again. But eventually his arguments and logic quieted her opposition, and he moved on to the next task.

Once the house was efficient, he applied his skills to the world of investment. He began to make investments that he believed to be safe but also held the potential for huge gains. Again Gina disagreed, but by now she knew she had no chance of succeeding.

She voiced her opinion but then withdrew in silence.

Phillip had now covered the key areas. He was well on the way to his goal of retirement at fifty. He would not have admitted he was a controller—he was only doing what to him was perfectly natural.

"I know that I will never be an adult with you"

Phillip's neat world shattered one evening when he came home and found Gina's clothes and much of the furniture moved out of the house and this note lying on the kitchen table:

> *Dear Phillip,*
>
> *I would like to be able to say I love you very much, but I'm not really sure what my feelings are at this point. We've been married for twenty-one years, and in the beginning we had some good years. But as time went on, I felt that you became more and more controlling. In recent years, I have felt that I am not a part of your life. You never ask my advice, and if I give it, you always tell me why I'm wrong. You've got the house running so efficiently that I can hardly get the soap off my back when I take a shower because the water is so weak. The wooden stove keeps me coughing constantly. I have decided that you can have your efficient house. I've got an apartment with plenty of water and fresh air.*
>
> *I know you see yourself as a solid husband. You probably wonder why I would do what I am doing. I guess that goes to show that you really haven't heard me through all these years. I have pleaded with you to let me be a part of your life, to treat me as an individual, to let my ideas count for something, but it has become obvious that the only ideas that matter in our marriage are your ideas. My feelings and my thoughts are unimportant. I thought for a long time*

that you were probably right—that I didn't have any good thoughts or good feelings. I know now that you are wrong. Everybody deserves the right to think and feel, and if they are married, to express those thoughts and feelings to their spouse and to be respected. I feel no respect from you. I feel that you have treated me as a child for many years. I'm tired of being a child; I want to be an adult. I know that I will never be an adult with you. So I'm leaving.

Don't expect me to come back. I've thought about this for a long time. I know that you will never change. Maybe you can't change. I hope you can retire at fifty, and I hope you find somebody who will enjoy your controlling personality. But that someone won't be me.

GINA

Phillip read the letter ten times that night. He was incredulous. He could not believe what he was reading. *What is she talking about—"controlling personality"?* he wondered. *I have done all of this for us. What is she talking about—treating her like a child? What does she mean—I didn't listen to her? I did listen, but I'm not going to do what she wants if I know it's not the best thing to do.*

Phillip knew there was no need to try to find her that night. He decided that he would get a good night's sleep, and tomorrow he would decide his strategy. He knew that he would come up with a plan, and if he could just talk to Gina, he could help her understand that she was wrong and needed to come home.

On his lunch hour he took his first step in his search-and-find strategy. He called his wife's best friend, knowing that she would know where Gina was. But the friend refused to tell him, so Phillip quickly shifted to Plan B. He told the friend how deeply hurt he was and how he could not believe what Gina had done. He emphasized how much he needed to talk to her and asked the friend to ask her if she would call him. The friend agreed, and Phillip felt that his first step had been somewhat successful.

However, Gina did not call that night, or the next. Phillip's search went on for a week, to no avail.

The next week, he received legal separation papers served to him by the local sheriff's department. Again, he sat at the kitchen table reading a document from Gina, this one far more formal, impersonal, and unemotional. He said to himself, *Doesn't she realize what she's doing? She is throwing it all away, and we are so close to our goal. How could she do this? She must be involved with someone else.*

He thought about this for a while and then called Gina's best friend. "Phillip, I can assure you she's not having an affair," the friend said. "I think if you will read her letter again you will understand why she's doing this. I think she has felt so controlled for so long that she found it emotionally unbearable."

The next day Phillip decided he would get a lawyer. *If this is what she wants, then I have to protect myself. Otherwise, she will take everything I've got.*

So the legal battle began between two lawyers. Over the next month, Phillip kept himself busy with work, keeping the house in order, and going to church meetings. He wanted everyone to know that this separation was not his idea, that he couldn't understand what had gotten into Gina.

Six weeks after Gina left, Phillip had still neither seen her nor heard from her. Then one night he was at the local Target when he looked up, and there she was. She saw him at the same time he saw her. He started walking toward her slowly, and when he was close enough he said, "Hi," and Gina responded, "Hi." They looked at each other in silence for what seemed like an eternity, and then Phillip said, "Gina, I don't know why you have chosen to do all this, but I do know that I still love you. Could we get together and talk?" To his surprise, she agreed.

On Friday night, they met for coffee. They shared with each other how things were going on their jobs. When they had caught up on each other's lives, Phillip launched into a lecture on on how "illogical" all of this was, on how they were going to lose everything he had worked for through all the years. He reminded her that this was not the Christian thing to do and expressed his concern about her faith in God.

Gina just stared at him. Then she said to him what she had wanted to say for many years. She poured out her pain of what it was like to live under his dominating influence. She told him that her life was being crushed out of her by his controlling behavior. She gave numerous examples. All the pain, the hurt, the frustration came back to her, and she was able to verbalize it to him. When she finished, Phillip was silent for a long time, and then he started shaking his head and said, "I never knew you felt that way," to which Gina responded, "I told you many times, Phillip. I told you *many* times."

"I guess I never really heard you," he said.

By this time, Gina said, "I think I need to go now."

As they stood outside Starbucks, Phillip said, "Gina, can't we work this out? I can change. Why don't you come home and let's work on it?"

"For many years, I hoped you would change, but you never did. It got worse instead of better. I can't live with you. It's not easy for you to change. If it was, you would have changed years ago."

Phillip didn't press the issue, but he did tell Gina that he appreciated her seeing him tonight and it was good to talk with her. They went to their separate cars and drove away in opposite directions.

Phillip: a process of self-discovery

Following this initial contact, Gina and Phillip met several times over the next few months. He always pleaded that she drop the separation and move home; Gina always insisted that there was no hope. Finally, one night she said, "Phillip, if you're really serious, then I'm going to suggest that you get counseling from someone who understands how to work with people who have controlling personalities, because even after all of our talks, I don't think you understand what I am saying. I'm not promising you that I will come back if you will get counseling; I am saying that I will *never* come back unless you get counseling."

Two weeks later, Phillip had an appointment with a counselor and began an extended process of self-discovery. He had never read books on psychology or relationships. But in a few weeks, he was discovering things about himself that he had never known, and he was beginning to understand why Gina had felt so controlled and oppressed. In due time, he was not only apologizing to his wife, but he was also sharing with her his insights about himself, and he was acknowledging that now he finally understood why she had taken the steps she had taken. He realized how oppressive his behavior had become. He told her that he would never try to

> *"I'm not promising you that I will come back if you will get counseling; I am saying that I will never come back unless you get counseling."*

force her to come back but that he would like to ask that they do some marriage counseling and see if there was any possibility of rebuilding their marriage.

After two weeks of thought, prayer, and talking with her own therapist, Gina agreed to begin marriage counseling. Seven months later, she and Phillip reaffirmed their vows to each other, and she moved back home. She had no sense that she was capitulating, nor did she have the sense that she had won a victory over Phillip. She did, however, have a deep confidence that, together, they had discovered not only the problems in their miserable marriage but also answers. Both of them had grown tremendously through the process, and she had every confidence that life together would be different in the future.

All this happened ten years ago, and Phillip and Gina now agree that it has been the happiest ten years of their lives. Neither of them is anticipating retirement. They are seeking to make the most of each day in their mutually supportive marriage.

Did Phillip lose his dominating personality? The answer is no, but he now understands it and understands that he must control his natural desires to dominate. He is also sensitive to how his actions affect others, especially Gina. It is not his desire to control her. She now has the freedom to share her emotions with him, and if she feels like he's trying to control her, she can share this with Phillip without fear of his response. She can predict that he will say, "Tell me about it. I want to understand what you are thinking and feeling." They are discovering how fulfilling a relationship can be when two people learn to respect each other, acknowledge differences, have genuine concern for the feelings and thoughts of the other, and seek to work together as a team for their mutual benefit.

Gina: tough love

Let me make two important observations about Gina's actions. Before taking the step to leave Phillip, she had been in counseling for four months. She shared with the counselor all the pain, frustration, and ambivalent feelings she had experienced through the years. She began to build her own self-confidence and sense of significance, which had been beaten down by Phillip's controlling behavior through the years. She was now emotionally strong enough to apply the principles of reality living. She took responsibility for her own attitude and realized that the way she thought would influence her actions. She knew that she could not change him, but she could influence him. All of her efforts at talking to him had been futile. She did not know that he would respond positively to her leaving, but she knew that she had to make that effort.

She understood that her actions should not be controlled by her emotions—the strongest of which was fear. *How will this affect the kids? What will people think? Can I make it financially?* If she had listened to her emotions, she would not have taken the hard step of tough love, but she knew that her emotions did not control her. She also acknowledged that she had not been a perfect wife and knew that her own imperfections did not mean that she was a failure or that her miserable marriage was her fault. Leaving Phillip was the most loving thing she knew to do. She prayed that the results would be positive. Most spouses who have lived with a highly controlling person for a long period of time will need the guidance of a counselor to take the kind of steps that Gina took.

My second observation is that a highly controlling person who has dominated a spouse for many years does not change quickly. Even after his wife left, Phillip's early efforts were aimed at manipulating her into coming home. At this point, he had almost no understanding of the problem. He was simply playing out the script of his personality: "If there is a problem, let's fix it." Gina did not yield to this pressure and gave him no hope of coming back. She had no assurance that Phillip would eventually understand and deal with his problem, but she knew that she could not settle for anything less than radical healing of the relationship.

HOW TO RESPOND TO A
CONTROLLING SPOUSE—AND HOW NOT TO

Are there actions less radical than separation that hold the potential for influencing a controlling spouse to make positive changes? The answer is yes. You should always try these actions first before taking the tough-love approach that Gina took.

Let's look first at two common negative approaches to a controlling spouse. The first is the power play. The attitude is, "Two people can play this game. If you are going to try to control me, I will fight you to the end." This approach leads to angry, heated arguments in which you try to out-argue your controlling spouse. The more the controller argues, the more you argue. No one ever wins, but the power play goes on. When the argument is over, you try to stay as uninvolved as possible over the next few days. Eventually, there is another power play, and the arguing continues. Many couples have followed this pattern for years.

The second negative approach is what I call the submissive-servant approach. The attitude is, "I yield to the controller and avoid conflict." The motto is "Peace at Any Price." This essentially renders you a slave to the controller's demands. Ironically, the submissive-servant approach does not make for peace. It simply plays out the battle inside you. Externally, you and your spouse seem to be at peace, but nothing could be further from the truth.

So what should you do to deal with a controlling spouse?

First, you must understand that the highly controlling person is one who has taken the need for freedom too far. The need for freedom is legitimate, but when your husband cares only for his own freedom with no concern for how it may take away from your freedom, he has become an abusive controller.

Second, you must understand and respond to the controller's need for *significance*. The self-worth of most controllers is tied to their performance. The more often they reach the tasks and goals they have set, the better they feel about themselves. The controlling wife interprets her failure to reach a goal as, "I am a failure." Thus, if you seek to influence your controlling wife, you must first address her inner needs for freedom and significance.

> *You will not argue well enough or long enough to influence a controller.*

It's important to remember that argument doesn't work with a controller. Arguing with a controller is like throwing gasoline on a fire. The controller is already strongly motivated to reach his/her goal. Your argument is simply one more obstacle in reaching that goal. It fires his engine to overcome your argument and prove that his way is the best way. You will not argue long enough or well enough to influence a controller.

The approach I have found most helpful is what I call *influencing by agreement*. You agree with the controller's arguments, but you don't allow yourself to be controlled by those arguments.

I hear someone objecting, "Agree with his arguments? I can't possibly do that." The reality is that you can almost always agree with the arguments of your spouse. Why? Because their arguments are correct—from *their* perspective. For example, all of Phillip's energy-conserving, money-saving ideas were correct from one perspective, namely, saving money. Therefore, the influence-by-agreement approach would lead Gina to say something like this: "Phillip, I really appreciate your efforts to save money. I think your goal to retire at fifty is a worthy goal. I'm sure that it will save some money to use the water-saver showerheads; but I can't afford to take thirty minutes to get the shampoo out of my hair. I want to help you save money, and if you will figure how much money we're saving by using the water-saver showerheads, I'll be happy to take that amount out of the food budget each month. From the money-saving perspective, it is a great idea, but from the practical perspective, it makes life really difficult for me."

If he persists with other arguments, Gina can agree with all of his arguments but insist that it is not a comfort that she is willing to sacrifice. If Phillip hasn't changed the showerhead in a week, she should have the old head reinstalled. Chances are he will mumble about how she's wasting money, but he will not reinstall the water-saving showerhead.

Influencing by agreement and yet not allowing yourself to be controlled hold tremendous potential for influencing a controlling spouse. First, this approach does not strike at the self-worth or significance of the controller. You are not arguing that his ideas are bad, which he will always interpret as personal criticism and will fight to prove that his ideas are worthy. Influencing by agreement virtually eliminates arguing rather than fueling its fire. It actually builds up your spouse's self-esteem because it affirms his purposes and agrees with his ideas.

However, it is extremely important to follow through with the second half of this approach and not allow yourself to be controlled by the controller. When you assert your own freedom to make decisions, you are helping your spouse understand by your actions that freedom is a two-way street. Once a controlling spouse sees that you have a mind of your own, they will likely come to respect your freedom.

Another approach that offers promise in positively influencing a controlling spouse is to *play to his or her strengths*. In the world of sports and business, good coaches and supervisors always follow this principle. The idea is to find the strengths of the player or employee and utilize these to the maximum. The principle also works in marriage and is especially helpful in influencing the controller. Since she is performance-oriented, she responds well to challenges to reach a given goal. Therefore, a controlling spouse will welcome a request for help: "You are really good at mapping out strategies to reach goals. Would you be willing to help me with a project? A friend of mine has asked me to come up with practical ideas on how she and her husband can enrich their marriage. I have some ideas, but would you give some thought to that, and next week we can pool our ideas?"

You may be surprised at the ideas the controller will produce. Ideas often include: reading and discussing a book on marriage, attending a marriage enrichment seminar, setting aside a time each day for conversation, having a date night once a week with each other, buying your spouse a gift even when there is no special occasion, taking walks together, expressing appreciation to each other, and so on. Once the list is made and you pass it on to your friend, you may begin trying to initiate some of these in your own marriage. Having been a part of the idea, the controller is far more likely to be willing to pursue such activities.

In summary, arguing and fighting with a controlling spouse is the worst possible approach. You can never win an argument with a controller; you only prolong the battle. Influencing by agreement and playing to his or her strengths are much more positive approaches. Both assume a kind but firm refusal to be controlled. Individuals who would be agents of positive change with a controlling spouse must accept responsibility for their own attitudes.

If these strategies of influencing your spouse do not lead to change, then the tough love approach Gina took with Phillip may be necessary. However, I would encourage you to work with a counselor before taking this step. You need someone to walk with you through this tough love approach. It is more likely to be successful if you have someone with whom you can share your thoughts, feelings, and actions on the journey.

It must also be acknowledged that not all tough love approaches lead to reconciliation. Remember, you can influence your spouse, but you cannot change your spouse.

FOR FURTHER HELP

- Andrea Bonior, PhD, "20 Signs Your Partner Is Controlling," *PsychologyToday.com,* June 01, 2015.
- Dr. Henry Cloud and Dr. John Townsend, *Boundaries in Marriage: Understanding the Choices That Make or Break Loving Relationships* (Grand Rapids: Zondervan, 2002).

8

The Verbally Abusive Spouse

You're an idiot. I don't know how anyone with your education could be as stupid as you are. You must have cheated to get your degree. If I were as stupid as you, I don't think I would get out of bed in the mornings."

The words seemed to beat on Laura relentlessly. This wasn't the first time Laura had heard such insults from her husband, Ron. The tragedy was that she had come to believe them. She was suffering from severe depression that literally kept her in bed most days. She was the victim of verbal abuse.

We have long known the devastation of physical abuse in a marriage relationship. (The next chapter will discuss responses to that kind of abuse.) We are now coming to understand that verbal abuse can be fully as devastating. Verbal abuse destroys respect, trust, admiration, and intimacy—all key ingredients of a healthy marriage.

Most of us lose our temper sometimes and may say harsh,

cutting words that we later regret. But if we are spiritually and emotionally mature, we acknowledge that this is inappropriate behavior. We express sorrow and ask forgiveness of our spouse, and the relationship finds healing.

The verbal abuser, on the other hand, seldom asks for forgiveness or acknowledges that the verbal tirades are inappropriate. Typically, the abuser will blame the spouse for stimulating the abuse. "She got what she deserved" is the attitude of the abuser.

Verbal abuse is warfare that employs the use of words as bombs and grenades designed to punish the other person, to place blame, or to justify one's own actions or decisions. Abusive language is filled with poisonous put-downs, which seek to make the other person feel bad, appear wrong, or look inadequate.

The verbal bombardment can be triggered by almost anything. A look, a tone of voice, a broken dish, or a crying baby can all pull the trigger on the arsenal of the verbal abuser. The verbally abusive spouse is out to punish, belittle, and control his or her partner. He or she does it compulsively and constantly, showing little empathy for the feelings of the spouse.

Verbal abuse is a contemporary term but an ancient malady. Solomon, the wise king of ancient Israel, wrote, "Fools give full vent to their rage."[1] King Solomon accurately understood the power of the tongue when he also said, "The tongue has the power of life and death."[2] Indeed, abusive words can bring death—death to the spirit and, if not corrected, death to the relationship. Those who have been verbally abused over long periods of time often say, "My emotions are dead. I used to feel hurt and anger; now all I feel is apathy."

Many abused spouses can identify with Janine, who said to her divorce lawyer, "I never knew what to do. He would always notice little things and then fly off the handle. If he saw that I put the roll of toilet paper on the holder with the paper going over rather than under, he'd lose it. It was always silly things. I tried arguing, I tried crying, I tried threatening divorce. Nothing seemed to get his attention. He blamed me for everything. It was always my fault. He was perfect. I don't know what else to do."

Is there hope for Janine and thousands of other spouses who suffer the barrage of verbal attacks as a way of life?

I believe there is, but that hope will not come in the form of a magic wand. It will be more like an exercise machine. It will require you to work hard and to be consistent. Progress will come slowly, but you will eventually experience the reward of your efforts.

BELIEVE IN YOUR OWN SELF-WORTH

In order to be a positive change agent, the spouse who is verbally abused must first recover a sense of their own self-worth. A wife whose husband has ridiculed her, threatened her, told her she is stupid, worthless, incompetent, a bad wife, and a failure as a mother may allow these messages to become self-fulfilling. As the verbal abuse increases, she may start to believe her husband. Eventually she may conclude that she does not deserve anything better and may give up any attempts to improve the situation. Her husband may tell her, "You ought to be thankful I keep you around because no one else would have you." She may come to believe what he says because there is no one else around to contradict his statements.

For this wife, the first step is to share her husband's abuse with a friend or counselor. She must first be able to reject these negative messages from her husband and rediscover her own self-worth. Only then can she become an agent of positive change in the marriage. If she does not deal with her own damaged self-esteem, she will not have the emotional energy to take constructive action with her husband.

UNDERSTANDING THE ABUSER

Most people who practice verbal abuse as a way of life are suffering from low self-esteem. Emotionally, the verbal abuser is not the strong, confident, self-assured individual he may appear to be. Inside he actually feels like a child, trying desperately to become an adult, fighting desperately but inappropriately to prove his worth. He is trying to bolster his own self-esteem by putting others down.

Many verbal abusers have an unconscious need to be seen as perfect. Social approval has become almost a holy quest for the verbal abuser. She often thinks that such approval requires perfection. Thus, any criticism jeopardizes her sense of approval. She explodes at the slightest criticism because it threatens her self-worth. That is why she must always win the argument; to acknowledge that she is less than perfect is to acknowledge her greatest fear—that she is, in fact, worthless.

The verbal abuser often grew up in a home with verbally abusive parents. He is expressing his anger in the same manner as his parents did. His problem is compounded by the fact that he has often stored his anger toward his parents but now releases that anger toward his spouse. Any solution for the verbal abuser must realistically address the whole problem of how to manage anger.

Of course there is always the possibility of mental illness or narcissistic personality disorder or NPS. NPS is characterized by exaggerated feelings of self-importance, an excessive need for admiration, and a lack of understanding others' feelings. Such people will need professional help if they are to break the pattern of verbal abuse.

BELIEVE IN THE WORTH OF YOUR PARTNER

Behind every verbally abusive tongue is a person of value. In spite of his or her devilish ways, your spouse bears the image of God and has innate value. It is this positive image that attracted you to your spouse before marriage. You saw something of value in his character and behavior. She met some of your own needs in the romantic stage of your relationship. Now it is time to remember that behind the facade of the verbally abusive lion to whom you are now married is the lamb that you used to cuddle. You married the lamb, not realizing that the lion would emerge. Now you must believe that the lamb is still there and that, with the help of God and others, the lamb can become predominant again. Your job is not to make the lamb return. Your job is to believe that it exists. It is the responsibility of your spouse to feed the lamb and starve the lion; however, your belief in the existence of the lamb may encourage your spouse to do his hard work.

On a quiet evening when Jeff had not yet unleashed a verbal attack, Marilyn said to him, "I've been thinking about us a lot the last few days. I've been remembering how kind you were to me when we dated. I'm remembering the tender touch, the kind words, the smiling face, the fun we had in those days. I guess that's why I believe in you so strongly. I know the good qualities you have inside. Sometimes I lose that vision when I am hurt by your attacks, but I know the kind of man you are, and I believe in that man. And I believe in my heart that the man I married is the man you really want to be. And I know that with God's help and your desire, you can reach that goal."

With those words, Marilyn is expressing belief in Jeff. She is giving him what all of us desperately want—someone to believe in us, someone to believe that we have good characteristics and that those good characteristics can flourish in our lives. Since the abuser is already suffering from low self-esteem, such comments build a positive sense of self-worth. If Jeff can come to believe in himself and believe that God's power is available to him, he may well return to being the man that Marilyn remembers.

SHARE YOUR OWN FEELINGS

Certainly you do not help an abusing spouse when you act as though the harsh words do not hurt you. The answer, however, is not to lash back, to retaliate with your own verbal abuse. The answer is to acknowledge that you have been wounded and need help. You need to remind your spouse that you are also human and that abusive words cut you deeply.

In the physical realm, there is a limit to the amount of pain you can endure before going to a physician. In the emotional sphere, the same is true. It is the inner pain from verbal abuse that may push you to talk to a counselor, a pastor, or a friend. But you should not hide from your spouse. He or she needs to live with an awareness that you are hurting and that your pain has led you to talk with someone. That fact may initially lead your spouse to further abuse, but ultimately it is a step toward healing.

In a contemplative mood, Mark said to Sharon, "There's something I really need to share with you. It is not easy for me to say it, but my pain is forcing me to talk. Over the last several weeks, I've really been hurting. I tried not to express it in front of the kids, and up until now, I've chosen not to share it with you. But the verbal attacks

In the physical realm, there is a limit to the amount of pain you can endure before going to a physician. In the emotional sphere, the same is true.

that I have heard from you have brought me tremendous pain. I am not sure how I should respond. I know that some of the things you say are true, and I would really like to work on those things. But I also think that some of the things you have said were spoken out of anger and are exaggerated. And I want you to know that I can't go on hearing your verbal attacks week after week without going for help.

"I really want to have a positive relationship with you," Mark continued. "But when I'm hurting so deeply, it's hard to be responsive. I've made an appointment with a counselor. I don't know if you want to go with me or not, but I've got to get help. I love you and I don't think that your behavior over the last month is characteristic of the real you. At the same time, I can't live with this any longer."

Mark is on the road to help, and perhaps Sharon will join him.

AGREE ON A STRATEGY

Once the problem of verbal abuse is laid on the table, you must develop a strategy for responding to the verbal bombshells. If your spouse is willing, you may work out the strategy together; or if you are going for counseling, the counselor can help you work out a strategy. If your spouse is unwilling to go for counseling and unwilling to talk with you about the problem, you must work out your own strategy and announce it to your spouse.

For example, Megan says to Barry in a context of calm, "I want to share with you a decision I've made. As you know, I have talked with you in the past about how deeply I am hurt when you lash out at me with critical and demeaning remarks. It takes me days and sometimes weeks to get over the pain that I feel on those occasions. I have decided that the next time you lose your temper and begin to yell at me, I will take some time away from you in order to recover. I think my healing will be faster if we are apart.

"I want you to know what I am doing. I will not be abandoning you, but I will be trying to take constructive action in what has become a very destructive pattern in our relationship. I can't survive your attacks indefinitely. I don't believe that is the kind of person you want to be. I know there is another person inside of you, and I believe in that person, and I believe that with God's help, you will become the good person that you and I both know you are.

"I'm sharing this with you because I believe in you and because I want you to know that I want to be as strong as I can to help you become the person you want to become."

Don't let verbal abuse "work." If you give in to your abusive spouse, you are encouraging the abuse.

Barry may immediately lash out, or he may be calm and express words of regret. Whatever his response, Megan will simply follow her plan the next time he explodes. Her time away with a friend or family member for two or three days will give him time to think and also help him realize the serious nature of his verbal abuse. If he abuses her verbally a subsequent time, Megan will repeat this strategy.

If this strategy does not move Barry to go for counseling, Megan will need to develop additional steps. It's important to have a plan and to follow the plan consistently.

Don't let verbal abuse "work." If you give in to your abusive spouse and do whatever the abuser is requesting, you are encouraging the abuse. You must never allow verbal abuse to work for the abuser. Typically, abusive patterns have succeeded in the past, and that is why they become entrenched. If you decide not to let them work, you are taking a positive step in breaking the pattern.

You could say to your spouse, "I have realized that in the past, I encouraged your verbal outbursts by caving in to whatever you desired of me. I realize now that this is wrong. I want you to know that in the future whenever you lash out at me in anger and verbally attack me, I will not be responsive to that kind of behavior. If you want to make a kind request of me as your spouse, I will certainly consider your request and may well do what you desire, but I will not encourage you to be a tyrant by giving in to you when you are ranting and raving." Having made such a statement, you must be consistent in following it.

PRACTICE THE POWER OF LOVE

Remember, the first principle of reality living requires you to take responsibility for your own attitudes. So as a verbally abused spouse, you must first of all refuse to believe the negative messages of your verbally abusing husband or wife. You must affirm your own worth in spite of the negative messages you are receiving from your spouse. Only as you come to see yourself as a person of worth and value will you be able to take positive steps that have the potential of changing your marriage relationships. Also, remind yourself that you cannot change your spouse's verbal behavior, but you can influence that behavior.

Understand that verbal abuse reveals the abuser's own low self-esteem and his or her inability to handle anger in a constructive way. Then you are free to have more constructive responses to the abuser's verbal outbursts.

Remember that your emotions must not control your actions. Your hurt, anger, or apathy may encourage you to give up, but you must choose instead to take constructive action, thus moving against your negative emotions. You must admit that you are not perfect, but your imperfections do not mean that you are a failure. Admitting your own failures, you are then free to choose the high road of loving your spouse unconditionally.

Reality living also recognizes the power of love as an agent for good. Unconditional love means that you will treat your spouse with kindness and respect even though he or she is not reciprocating. Remember, love is not a feeling; it is an attitude with appropriate behavior. It is the attitude that says, "I choose to look out for your interests. How may I help you?" This does not mean that love puts up with abusive behavior. It is interesting that even God in the New Testament Scriptures, while loving, chooses to discipline; in fact, His love motivates Him to discipline His children.[3] Love sometimes must be tough. Love holds a spouse accountable for inappropriate behavior.

Love says, "I care about you too much to sit here and let you destroy me and yourself. I know that is not for your good, and I will not cooperate in the process." Love takes constructive action for the benefit of the loved one regardless of how difficult the action may be.

Do the above suggestions guarantee that your spouse will change his or her abusive behavior? Unfortunately, I can give you no such guarantee. You cannot determine another's choices. You can, however, make wise choices. You can be a responsible person even when your spouse is being irresponsible. Remember, you are not responsible for your spouse's behavior. You are responsible for your own behavior. You did not make your spouse a verbal abuser, but you do choose what your response will be to that abuse. Retaliation (fighting fire with fire), capitulation (giving up and becoming a doormat), and denial (acting as though nothing is wrong) are all common responses to verbal abuse. None of them, however, is a healthy response.

TAKING THE HIGH ROAD IN IOWA

I met Dale at one of my marriage seminars in Iowa. He was a pig farmer and extremely successful in his business. "If raising pigs and making money could ensure a good marriage," he said, "I would have one."

He went on to explain, "I consider myself a strong man. I don't usually let things get me down, but my wife's constant criticism has almost destroyed me. Other people can get on my case, and I let it roll off like water off a pig's back, but when my wife constantly criticizes me it is like a dagger in my heart.

"She's so negative, not only toward me but toward everyone and toward life in general. She stays depressed a lot of the time . . . Her life is miserable, and she tries to make my life miserable. I find myself wanting to stay away from the house and not be around her. I know that's not the answer. It has affected our sex life and everything. I don't want to leave my wife. I know she needs help, but I don't know how to help her."

After hearing Dale's story, I strongly urged him to seek counseling on how he could become an agent of positive change in his marriage. He countered that the nearest counselor was fifty miles away. I assured him that it would be worth the drive.

Two years later, I was greatly encouraged when I returned to Iowa for another marriage seminar and saw Dale again. (He had driven one hundred fifty miles to attend the seminar.) This time his wife was with him, and at one of our break times he told me what had happened over the past two years.

Dale's first discovery in the counseling process was finding out why his wife's critical words had been so painful to him. Two factors gave him this insight.

The first discovery that helped him came from recalling his family of origin. Dale had absorbed a lot of critical words from his family, growing up. He could never do anything to his father's satisfaction. Thus, Dale grew up with the feeling of inadequacy. As a boy, the message playing in his mind ran something like: When I get to be a man, I will be a success. I will prove my dad wrong, and I will get recognition. In adulthood, Dale had lived out that dream. His hard work and commitment had paid off; he was a successful farmer and was known not only in the county but also in the state. He was indeed respected by his peers, but the person whose affirmation he most desired, namely, his wife, only echoed his father's condemning messages. What he had worked all his life to overcome was staring him in the face every day.

The second insight that helped Dale understand himself was the discovery that his primary love language is words of affirmation. The thing that genuinely makes him feel loved and appreciated is hearing affirming words. Thus, his wife was speaking a hostile, foreign love language as she gave him condemnation instead of affirmation. Her words stung more deeply because he was suffering from an empty love tank. Her critical words were like bullets piercing the love tank itself. He was emotionally devastated.

Dale also discovered something about his wife's needs. Erika was operating out of her own unmet emotional needs. He learned that her primary love language was quality time, and that because of the long hours required on the farm and his strong desire to be a successful farmer, he had little time left over for her. In the earlier days of the marriage, Erika had begged him to spend time with her, to take her to a movie, to attend the church picnic with her, to take a vacation in the summer, to spend two days in Chicago just having fun. But he had been too busy for such things.

Now he realized that he had not spoken his wife's primary love language for years. And he now realized that her critical words were desperate cries for love. Erika's verbal abuse had grown out of her sense of hopelessness in the marriage, and her growing lack of interest in their sexual relationship was stark evidence that she felt little emotional love coming from him.

"I finally got it," Dale said. "So I was able to help Erika. I shared with her that I was learning a lot about myself and about marriage from my counselor. I told her that I recognized that in many ways I had not been a good husband and that with God's help I wanted to change that.

"She was shocked the morning I told her that I would like for us to go on a picnic at the lake near us," he said. "She couldn't believe it. But when I came in from the morning chores and started taking a shower, she started packing the picnic. We spent three hours together, walking, sitting, and talking. I told her how sorry I was that I had spent so little time with her through the years and that I wanted us to make the future different. She opened up and told me her pain from past years and reminded me of the times she had begged for my attention. But this time she wasn't being critical, just honest about her need for love. Toward the end of the afternoon, we found ourselves hugging and kissing. It almost seemed like we were dating again."

Over the next couple of months, Dale planned several other quality-time experiences with his wife, and each evening he spent time talking and listening to her as they discussed the day's events. He noticed that she was spending less time in bed each day and that she began to be more sexually responsive. In time, her whole countenance changed. The flow of critical words slowed and then eventually stopped.

Erika went on to read my book *The 5 Love Languages* and recognized immediately that Dale's primary love language is words of affirmation. Now that her own love tank was filled by the quality time she had received from him, it was easier for her to give Dale the words of affirmation he craved.

Erika joined Dale at the next marriage seminar and told me what the changes meant to her: "He went for counseling and our marriage has totally changed. I am excited that we can come to the seminar together this year. I know that I am going to learn some things that will help both of us."

Dale had discovered firsthand that although we cannot change our spouses, our positive actions can have a profound, positive influence on their behavior.

FOR FURTHER HELP

- Susan Titus Osborn and Karen L. Kosman, *Wounded by Words: Healing the Invisible Scars of Emotional Abuse* (Birmingham, AL: New Hope Publishers, 2008).
- Leslie Vernick, *The Emotionally Destructive Marriage: How to Find Your Voice and Reclaim Your Hope* (Colorado Springs: WaterBrook, 2013).

9

The Physically Abusive Spouse

Domestic violence, or intimate partner violence, affects millions of women and men each year. It may include physical abuse, sexual abuse, threat of physical or sexual abuse, and emotional abuse.[1] The results of such abuse are devastating, not only to the one abused but also to the children who grow up in such homes. The results are often deadly—it is estimated that around 4,000 women die annually due to domestic violence.[2]

In this chapter, we will focus on the physically abusive spouse. Physical abuse is any act that inflicts bodily harm or is intended to do so. It may consist of hitting, shoving, kicking, choking, throwing objects, or using a weapon. The severity of physical abuse can range from a slap across the face to homicide. If verbal abuse can kill the spirit, physical abuse can eventually kill the person.[3]

Researchers have discovered certain patterns as to when and where spousal abuse occurs. Most abuse happens between the hours of 6:00 p.m. and 6:00 a.m. The typical location of physical abuse is in the victim's home.[4]

THE CYCLE OF ABUSE

Research has shown a three-phase cycle in physical abuse.[5] First is *the tension-building phase*. This is the period in which the abuser experiences a series of irritations. His frustration with them escalates, and he keeps his feelings inside. As the feelings become more intense, he will verbally express his hostility. At this point, the wife may attempt to placate her husband, trying to calm him and avoid further confrontations. This may work temporarily, but the tension continues to build inside the abuser. He then expresses further angry verbal responses. When the wife feels there is no hope of placating him, she tends to withdraw. The husband sees her withdrawal and reacts with even more intense anger. This phase of building tension may last anywhere from an hour to several months.

Next comes *the explosion phase*, when physical abuse actually occurs. The abuser now unleashes his aggressive behavior toward his spouse. This phase ends when the battering stops. With it comes a reduction in the amount of tension.

The third phase is remorse, often called the "honeymoon phase." After the explosion, there is a period of relative calm. The abusive spouse may apologize profusely, show some kindness to the wife, and promise that the abuse will never happen again. Such behavior often comes out of a sense of guilt over the harm inflicted as well as fear of losing a spouse. During this phase, the abusive spouse may really believe that he will never, never express violence again. The partner often wants to believe him and thus remains in the relationship. During this "makeup" time, the relationship may be better than at any other period in their lives; but eventually the abusive spouse will become irritated again. The tension will begin to build, and the cycle will be repeated.

Beth said about her abusing husband, "He seems so sincere when he apologizes. He even has tears in his eyes. He admits that what he did was wrong. He asks me to please forgive him and promises that it will never happen again. He seems so sincere I want to believe him, but every time it happens again." It was obvious that the abuse cycle was strongly established in his behavior.

WHY DOES SHE PUT UP WITH IT?

In the vast majority of the cases, it is the husband who abuses the wife; however, there are cases where wives physically abuse husbands.[6] The abuse typically continues for months, even years. In fact, studies indicate that the more severe the abuse, the longer it takes the abused woman to leave her partner.[7] Why do battered wives wait so long to take action? Let's look at some of the common factors.

Typically, the initial episodes of violence begin during the first year of marriage. In the beginning, the wife may blame herself, thinking that if she had acted differently her spouse would not have gotten violent. The first several episodes are infrequent. The husband is usually remorseful and the wife forgiving. As his explosions come more often, her belief in his apologies evaporates. Quite often by the time she realizes

Some battered wives are rescuers. They find their self-worth in helping those in need.

the abuse is serious, she feels overwhelmed and helpless. Many battered wives grew up in homes where there was a measure of physical violence. So in the early stages, she is somewhat accepting of her husband's abusive behavior. She may also suffer from low self-esteem, acquired in her own childhood. If this is the case, she will tend to blame herself for her husband's explosions, and she will seek desperately to meet his needs and to keep him happy.

Some battered wives are rescuers. They find their self-worth in helping those in need. Many wives of abusive husbands were first drawn to their spouses because of the man's need for someone to nurture him. The wife often enjoys the relationship when the abuse is not occurring. She bonds to the warmer side of her husband because he still meets some of her need to be loved.

Another reason some abused wives procrastinate in taking action against their husband's abuse is that they have isolated themselves. Kim is a good example. When I asked why she had not shared her abusive situation with her extended family, she said, "I didn't want them to know that we had problems. Before we got married, my mother told me that I should not marry Kevin. I guess she saw something I didn't see. I was ashamed to tell her what was going on. I would stay away until my bruises healed; sometimes I didn't have contact with my family for weeks except on the phone." Kim also indicated that she had dropped out of her class at the local community college where she was trying to learn coding. Her reasoning was the same—she didn't want anyone to know that she was having problems. Such isolation keeps the battered spouse from finding the help she needs.

Fear is another factor that keeps abused wives from taking action. They know what their husbands have done in the past, and they are afraid that if they contact family, a pastor, a friend, or the police, the abuse will become even worse. These wives are often emotionally dependent on their husbands. After years of abuse, they have little self-confidence. Their security is in the familiar. The prospect of disrupting family life and their security is more than they can bear. They also may depend on their husbands for finances. Even if they are working outside the home, chances are they do not believe that they could live on their salary. Thus, their emotional or economical dependency on their husbands keeps them in the prison of fear.

I first met Jennifer a year before she married Mitch. She was a happy though timid twenty-one-year-old. She came to me to discuss her problems with self-esteem. She had fallen in love with Mitch, although her family did not particularly care for him. She admitted that he was sometimes "rather blunt," but she understood that "it was just his way." She wanted desperately to get married and believed that he was her man. After marriage, they moved rather soon out of town where Mitch secured a better job. Ten years later, when I encountered Jennifer at one of my marriage seminars held in her city, she was a young mother riddled with fear. She told me her story of physical abuse so severe that she had been to the hospital emergency room three times in the last two years. Her parents knew nothing of what was going on. She did not have a job and had no friends. Financially she saw no hope of making it without Mitch. She was virtually a prisoner in her own house, feeling desperate and helpless. Many battered spouses can identify with Jennifer.

Is there hope for the thousands of Jennifers who suffer physical abuse from their husbands? Does reality living offer any genuine hope? I believe the answer to those questions is yes. An abused wife can become an agent for positive change in the marriage, but I do not believe that she can do it alone. She will need the help of a trained counselor, the support of family or friends, and she will need to draw upon her spiritual resources.[8]

JULIE: REACHING OUT

Julie was sitting in my office wearing dark glasses and a long-sleeved sweater. It was mid-June. The sun was shining brightly outside. The sunglasses would not have been out of place, but in North Carolina you don't need a long-sleeved sweater in mid-June. She took off her glasses and didn't say a word. I knew I was in the presence of a battered woman. Her eye was black, and later I saw that her arms had turned blue from bruises inflicted by her enraged husband.

"Dr. Chapman, I've got to have help," she said. "My husband lost control. He hit me with the telephone repeatedly, and he threw a Coke bottle at me. I can't live like this," she said.

"Has anything like this happened before?" I asked. The answer was what I expected.

She feared telling friends at church, ashamed of what was going on in her home.

"Yes, it's happened several times before, but I've never shared it with anyone until now. He always tells me he's sorry and it won't happen again. And I want to believe him, but it does happen again. This time is the worst, and I know that I can't take any more chances. I should not have let it go on this long. I need help in deciding what to do."

In further conversation with Julie, I discovered that she had grown up in a home where her father physically abused her mother. Julie's father had never physically abused her, but he had frequently abused her verbally. She still remembered the day her father told her that she was a loser, that she was just like her mother, and that he pitied the man who would marry her. Now I understood why, for the first twelve years of their marriage, Julie had taken Bruce's abuse as something she deserved. She was living out her father's prophecy.

Julie had told no one about the abuse because of fear. She feared telling her parents because she didn't want to hear her father say, "You got what you deserved." And she knew in her heart that her mother had no answers to physical abuse. She feared telling her employer, thinking she might lose her job. She feared telling friends at church, ashamed of what was going on in her home. Now this most recent episode, the most violent of all, had finally pushed her to reach out for help.

She entered my office convinced that divorce was her only hope, yet she saw no way to leave Bruce. She knew that financially she and her six-year-old son could not live on her salary. She knew that asking her parents for financial assistance would bring her nothing but condemnation. She saw no way to survive apart from Bruce, yet she knew that she could not endure further abuse. She feared that if she left, he would kill her or harm their son. Julie exhibited many of the common characteristics of an abused wife: low self-esteem, isolation, a sense of helplessness, fear, and financial dependence on her husband.

As a counselor, I knew that she had to deal with these issues before she would have the emotional strength to take positive action in her marriage. I hoped that we could make some progress in these areas before the next violent episode erupted. Julie indicated that usually after an explosion, things would be rather calm for two or three months before Bruce exploded again. I told her that I would be willing to help her if she would make a commitment to work with me for one year and, to the best of her ability, do the things that I recommended. "Dr. Chapman, I'm willing to do anything," she replied. "I've got to have help."

I made three requests of Julie that first session. First, I asked that she agree to meet with me once a week for the next three months while we worked on helping her get to the place where she could take some constructive action in her marriage. Second, I asked her to begin attending a local spouse abuse support group. I knew that in this group she would learn to tell her story to others and find encouragement and support. I also knew that in the group she would learn about the local shelter for battered women, a place where she could go twenty-four hours a day. Finally, I requested that she read the book *The Search for Significance*,[9] which deals with understanding the basis of self-esteem. She agreed and consistently followed through with all three requests.

Important: If this pattern of abuse is happening to you, please remove yourself and your loved ones from the situation as soon as possible and get some help. For immediate help and counsel call: 1-800-799-SAFE (7233).

FEAR—AND ACTION

By the end of the three months, Julie was coming to see herself in a totally new light. She recognized that she was a person of worth, that she had average intelligence and was as capable as the next person. She was coming to understand that she was responsible for her own attitudes and behavior, and that while she could not change Bruce's behavior, she could influence his behavior by her own actions. She was also coming to understand that while verbalizing her emotions to me and to her support group was extremely important, she need not let her emotions control her behavior. Even with feelings of fear, she could still take positive actions. In short, she had laid the foundation for reality living.

According to Julie, Bruce had been fairly calm during the

first two months following the last explosion. But by the third month, she was beginning to feel the tension building within him. He was becoming more and more verbally critical of her and would get upset at the smallest irritation. We both felt that the possibility of another explosion was imminent. I felt it was time for Julie to take the tough-love approach to Bruce's abusive behavior. Some of her fears resurfaced. "I know in my heart that you are right," she said, "but I'm still fearful of what he will do."

I was sympathetic with her fear because I knew that it was based in reality. There was every possibility that if she took action to seek to influence his behavior, Bruce was likely to become physically violent.

However, if she took no action, he would also become physically abusive. We both agreed that the tough-love approach was better than the "wait and get hit" approach.

In the support group, Julie had met a woman who was separated from her husband and looking for a roommate with whom she could share the rent. After talking with the support group leader, I agreed with Julie that this was a good place for her to stay, at least for a few weeks or months. I suggested that she write a letter to Bruce, telling him her pain and frustration from the past abuse and letting him know that she loved him too much to remain in the relationship and let him destroy her and ultimately himself; that she had decided the best thing for her to do was to move out until he could find an answer to his abusive explosions. I also encouraged her to indicate her willingness to work on their marriage after Bruce had extensive counseling to help him learn how to deal with his anger and frustration, but that until he got such help, she could no longer stay in the home.

Julie wrote the letter. At the end of the letter, she noted that if Bruce wanted counseling, he could call my office. She wrote down my phone number for him. Friends in the support group agreed to help her move her things out of the house, and she left Bruce the letter on the kitchen table.

BRUCE: ANGRY, REMORSEFUL

Bruce's response was immediate. Before my admin arrived in the office the next morning, he had left a message on her voice mail asking for an appointment with me. Four days later, he was in my office. He was angry, remorseful, frustrated, and "willing to do anything to get Julie back."

I told Bruce that I was glad he had come to see me. I told him that I hoped his dream of his wife coming back could someday be realized, and I told him that I believed she was open to that. I also told him that this would not happen next week or next month. I told him that I was proud of Julie for the actions she had taken, because I thought it was a genuine expression of her love for him. I explained that if he loved her and wanted his marriage to be restored, he would have to do the hard work of learning how to deal with anger and how to love her more effectively.

"That process will take weeks and maybe months," I said. "But if you're willing, I'd be glad to refer you to a colleague who specializes in helping men like you. I will keep in touch with the counselor, and whenever the counselor feels that it's time to talk about reconciling the marriage, I will be happy to work with you and Julie on that process."

Then I warned Bruce that any effort to contact Julie or to abuse her physically would jeopardize his possibility of restoring their relationship. "This is not a time for retaliation but rather a time for personal growth in your life," I suggested. "The counselor I am referring you to has a support group for men who have physically abused their wives. Become a part of that group, Bruce. I believe your progress will be faster if, beyond individual counseling, you participate with the group." I knew that my colleague would also suggest this, but I wanted to plant the seed in Bruce's mind so he would have time to think about it.

The next week Bruce began his counseling, and the following week he enrolled in the support group. He was not 100 percent successful in following my suggestion that he make no contact with Julie for at least a month. Three times in the first month, he tried to make contact with her. Once he tried to call her at her work; once he was in the parking lot when she got off from work and hoped to talk to her. Fortunately, she had a friend walking with her to the car, and Bruce did not make contact, although she saw him and he saw her. His third attempt to contact Julie was at her office, which created somewhat of a scene until her supervisor asked Bruce to leave. She reported each of these incidents to me. I, in turn, shared these with Bruce's counselor. The counselor confronted Bruce and affirmed that this was not the way to restore his marriage, that in due time we would arrange for him to have a conversation with Julie, but that for now he needed to concentrate on his own personal growth and understanding.

Over the next four months, Bruce's counselor and support group helped him to understand that expressing anger in an abusive manner is a learned behavior and that it can be unlearned; that he must take responsibility for his violent outbursts; that such outbursts are never constructive; and that he must learn constructive ways to process his anger. Bruce also began to recognize that violence is never justified in a marriage and that uncontrolled expressions of anger must be stopped if the marriage is to continue. He learned how to recognize when tension started to build up inside and also how to process minor irritations before they got to the explosive state.

Bruce came to understand that much of his behavior was motivated by his own low self-esteem and was, in fact, an effort to prove his worth. He also realized that such efforts were never successful and that each explosion led to a greater sense of incompetence. He learned and practiced with his support group methods for resolving conflict.

The basic goal in treating abusive spouses is not to eliminate anger but to replace abusive expressions of anger with positive expressions. One advantage of group therapy is that group members tend to confront each other more directly and perhaps more effectively than the therapist. Hearing other men in a support group say, "I don't like what I'm doing, and I want to stop," is a powerful model for an abuser. The group experience also helps men overcome some of their emotional isolation from other men. After a group is established, members often will reach out to other members during times of crisis. Such a support group for abusing husbands serves much the same role as an Alcoholics Anonymous group does for alcoholics.

COUNSELING—OR ELSE

After several weeks, Bruce's counselor arranged for a joint meeting with Bruce and Julie. The discussion, however, was not related to restoring their marriage. The session dealt with how they had handled anger in the past and how they anticipated handling anger in the future. In this session, Julie assured Bruce that if he could learn to handle his anger and that if they could learn how to love and support each other, she was willing to discuss the possibility of restoring their marriage. This gave Bruce the needed encouragement to continue the counseling process. For most men, the strongest external motivator to get counseling is the desire to keep their wives. This is often the only way that men will reach out for counseling. Their wives have said, "You participate in counseling or else." Eventually, these men will internalize this motivation in a sincere desire to change what they finally realize is inappropriate behavior. Few abusing husbands will go for counseling without such pressure. It is important that the wife not return to the home too soon and thus remove this strong motivator for her husband to continue counseling.

It was nine months after Bruce started his counseling that we all agreed that it was time for Julie and Bruce to begin marriage counseling. I began seeing them weekly for one month and bimonthly for the next two months. At the end of three months of marriage counseling, we agreed it was time for Julie to move home. She had been away for a little over a year. During the three months I was counseling with this couple, they had a dinner date once a week. Thus, Julie had not only our counseling sessions to give her confidence, but also the realization that she could be with Bruce alone and that they could talk without angry outbursts.

HOME AGAIN

Julie moved back home with confidence, and I continued to counsel with them every two weeks for the next three months, and once a month for the following six months. During this time, they attended a three-month marriage enrichment clinic offered by a local church, which met once a week and had homework assignments. They both realized that a happy marriage is something that requires regular attention, and they committed themselves to a pattern of growth.

My last session with Bruce and Julie was eight years ago, but I have continued to keep in contact with them from time to time. They have consistently followed two suggestions that I gave them in our final session. One was to attend a marriage enrichment event every year. Some years this is a weekend retreat; other years, this is a class that runs for six or eight weeks. And the second suggestion was to read and discuss a book on marriage once a year.

These are two practical ways for keeping a healthy marriage invigorated. In the eight-plus years that Bruce and Julie have been back together, he has never physically harmed her. They have had the normal misunderstandings and conflicts, which they have had to process. Sometimes they have raised their voices and felt anger toward each other, but they have learned how to call "time-out" until the anger subsides and they can resolve the conflict.

The fact that they both dealt responsibly with the problem of physical abuse and have learned how to relate to each other in a healthy manner has built up self-esteem in both of them. Bruce and Julie have shared with friends that the crisis centering on his physical abuse has been the biggest learning experience in their lives. Both of them shudder to think what might have happened if Julie had not taken the tough-love approach in response to Bruce's abuse. They now lead workshops on anger management in a marriage enrichment class sponsored by their church. Who could be more qualified to lead such a group?

Let me briefly summarize how Julie applied the principles of reality living.

First of all, she recognized that she is responsible for her own attitude. Before counseling, her attitude was, "I am in an abusive marriage and my only hope is divorce." In counseling, her attitude shifted to, "I am in an abusive marriage, and I will use this to gain self-understanding." Later her attitude became, "I understand why I have been passive in dealing with my abusive husband. I will now seek to discover positive actions I can take to address this situation." Clearly this new attitude began to affect her actions.

Julie also came to understand that she could not change Bruce's behavior, but that there were positive actions she could take that held the potential for influencing his behavior. She understood that her negative emotions did not have to control her actions.

She took positive actions even when she had feelings of fear and uncertainty. Such actions did, in fact, have a positive effect on his behavior. They motivated him to get the counseling he needed to gain the self-awareness and understanding necessary to make positive changes in his life. She demonstrated that love is the most powerful weapon for

Will tough love always motivate the abuser to get help? The answer is no.

good in the world, even if that love must be tough love. Together, she and Bruce learned how to help meet each other's emotional needs for love, freedom, significance, self-worth, recreation, and, eventually, peace with God.

Putting these principles to work with an abusive spouse does not always produce such satisfying results, but it does always stimulate growth in the life of the person who chooses to practice reality living.

I want to say once again that I do not believe a spouse who has been abused over a long period of time will be able to take such constructive actions without the help of professional counseling. I urge you, if you are in an abusive marriage, to seek such counseling immediately. It will be worth the time, effort, and money you spend and will offer the greatest potential for a positive outcome in your desperate marriage.

The ideal time to deal with a physically abusive spouse is the first time such abuse happens. Normally at this stage in the marriage the wife has the emotional maturity to say, "I love you very much, but I will not live with you until you get counseling and learn how to handle your anger." Because the marriage is young and the husband does not want to lose his wife, he may well respond positively to her request. However, if he does not move to get counseling then she should see a counselor and begin to apply tough love sooner rather than later. Many wives could have spared themselves years of pain by applying reality living early in the marriage.

However, many young wives have not read books on physical abuse early in the marriage because they never anticipated such abuse. Thus they only reach out for help after suffering numerous abusive episodes. These are the wives who will need a counselor to help them regain their sense of self-worth and the emotional energy to practice tough love. Will tough love always motivate the abuser to get help? The answer is no. That is why moving out as an act of tough love may lead to permanent separation. Living apart is a better alternative than subjecting yourself (and perhaps your children) to the destructive behavior of an abuser.

FOR FURTHER HELP

- *Important*: If this pattern of abuse is happening to you, please remove yourself and your loved ones from the situation as soon as possible and get some help. For immediate help and counsel call: **1-800-799-SAFE (7233)**.
- thehotline.org: Extensive resources and information on intimate partner abuse, including connections to local organizations and shelters

The Sexually Abused/Sexually Abusive Spouse

I met Justin during a weekend marriage enrichment retreat held in the beautiful Colorado Rockies. He was an outdoorsman and seemed full of life. But behind closed doors, he shared his heart.

"Dr. Chapman, my wife, Sarah, and I have been married for fifteen years now, and we have a fairly good marriage. She's a good woman and a good mother, but there's one area of our marriage that we've never been able to solve. Sarah has almost no interest in sex. In fact, she is fairly resistant to any sexual desire that I express. She says that she just doesn't feel comfortable with anything sexual. She won't even allow me to fondle her breasts. Dr. Chapman, is that normal?"

I could tell that Justin was hurting deeply. I cut to the heart of the matter with my next question. "Do you know if Sarah was sexually abused as a child?" He nodded and said, "Yes. That all came out several years ago. She shared it with me and then with our pastor. We prayed about it, and I think she forgave her father. We didn't talk about it much after that." Justin and Sarah were experiencing the painful residue of childhood sexual abuse. Unfortunately, thousands of couples can identify with their problem.

Sexually abused children eventually become adults. Many of them will marry and discover that time did not heal the scars. In this chapter we will walk behind closed doors and observe two painful realities related to sexual abuse: first, the pain of living with a spouse who was sexually abused as a child; and second, the pain of discovering that your husband has sexually abused your children. In both situations emotions run deep, and pain lingers long. Answers seem elusive, and frustration often reigns. Sexuality is at the heart of our humanity, and when it is distorted in childhood, it poisons the root systems of our relationship skills as adults.

Can reality living help us untangle the twisted wires of sexual identity and find marital intimacy? I believe the answer is yes, but the process will take time, patience, and, most likely, the help of a professional counselor. Reality living begins with the affirmation that *sexual abuse is morally wrong and has devastating emotional and physical effects on the abused person.* By sexual abuse, I mean any sexual activity—verbal or physical—that is forced on another individual without his or her consent, which uses him or her as an object to meet another person's sexual desires. Such an act perpetrated on a child sets in motion a whole series of emotional and physical reactions that have a detrimental effect on a child's normal sexual maturation process.

This distortion of sexuality follows the child to adulthood and often causes problems in the marital relationship. These victims of sexual abuse will often find it extremely difficult to enjoy healthy sexual interaction with their spouses. Many are filled with shame, guilt, fear, anger, and often revulsion toward sex. These deep-seated emotions are often accompanied by the inability to enjoy kissing, touching of breast or penis, and often an aversion to looking at a naked body, including one's own. The person does not desire to have these negative emotions related to sexual matters but finds it impossible to feel differently. Thus, we are dealing with an extremely serious roadblock to a physically intimate marriage.

SARAH: BEYOND SILENCE

Often a person successfully hides the sexual abuses of childhood. In fact, the wife or husband of an abused spouse may not even suspect it. Let's return to Justin.

"Were you aware of the fact that Sarah had been sexually abused by her father before you were married?" I asked Justin during a break at the Rocky Mountain seminar.

"No," he said, "and that's part of what bothers me. Before we were married, she seemed to be sexually responsive. In fact, we were sexually active before we got married. It was a year or two into the marriage before Sarah started drawing back from sexual involvement. If the sexual abuse was the problem, I don't understand why she could have been sexually responsive before marriage and in the early days of our marriage. That's why I've never felt her childhood sexual abuse was the problem."

I shared with Justin that one of the common characteristics of females who have been sexually abused is that in adulthood they often have ambivalent feelings toward sex. At times, they can feel that the only way to be loved is to be sexually active. Sometimes they are active with several partners, but at other times, they draw back from sex and want nothing to do with it. In marriage, this ambivalence can be very frustrating. On a given day, a wife may make comments that lead her husband to believe that she is interested in being sexually intimate. She may even flirt with him, but when it comes to the actual time of foreplay and intercourse, she becomes a stone.

> *She was tormented by such thoughts as I'm a failure . . . People will betray me . . . My body is ugly.*

"Yes," Justin interrupted. "That's exactly the way Sarah is some days."

"Victims of sexual abuse often suffer from bouts of depression in which they withdraw not only from sex but also from life itself," I continued. Justin was nodding yes. "They often suffer from low self-esteem and will make negative comments about themselves. They seldom express it, but they often feel a sense of hopelessness—that life will not get better and, in fact, that 'I do not deserve a good life.' As a victim of childhood sexual abuse, they often bear the load of shame and guilt. Victims feel guilty even though the abuse was not their fault."

What Sarah had inside were a lot of mixed emotions and many false ideas about what happened to her and the results of that abuse, I explained. She was tormented by such thoughts as *I'm a failure . . . I can never be close to anyone . . . People will betray me . . . My body is ugly . . . Sex is something that is taken from me . . . I'll never be able to forgive my father, and I'll never be able to forgive myself.*

"These false impressions, coupled with the emotions of guilt, shame, betrayal, and sometimes denial have held her in bondage for many years. It is like a cancer eating away at her emotional and spiritual well-being. She will not be healed without help," I said.

I could tell that what I was saying made sense to Justin, and that he was beginning to realize that he had underestimated the impact of Sarah's childhood sexual abuse on her behavior throughout their marriage. I said, "The devastating results of sexual abuse are seldom ever removed by one visit to a pastor. That is a starting place, but it is only the first step of many. If Sarah is to find healing from the pain of sexual abuse, and if the two of you are to find sexual intimacy, she will need your support, God's help, and the guidance of a caring counselor. Few people ever find genuine healing without these three ingredients."

I gave him the name of a counselor near his hometown and suggested that, if Sarah were willing, they should initiate the counseling together as soon as possible. Justin was ready, and he hoped that Sarah would be willing.

After the break, the seminar resumed. When we came to the section on sexual intimacy, I noticed that Justin's wife seemed somewhat uncomfortable. But at the end of the session, she sought me out and asked the simple question, "Dr. Chapman, is there any hope for someone who has been sexually abused as a child? I want to experience the kind of positive sexual relationship that you described, but it seems almost impossible."

I tried to communicate my sympathetic feelings for her struggle. Having worked with so many people in her situation through the years, I know that it's easy to lose hope. I assured Sarah that there could be healing for past pain and that she could grow to have a healthy sexual relationship with her husband. I recommended a book, *Beyond the Darkness: Healing for Victims of Sexual Abuse*,[1] and told her that most people would need counseling to find ultimate healing.

Two years later, I was encouraged when I got a letter from

Justin telling me that he and Sarah had read the book, discussed it together, and agreed to seek counseling. "It has been the greatest learning experience of our lives," he said.

EXTRACTING THE PAIN

"Neither of us knew anything about the impact of sexual abuse," Justin continued. "I am saddened to think that Sarah suffered silently from the pain of being betrayed by her father for all those years. I realized that I had focused on my own disappointment in our sexual relationship and had not understood the impact of the abuse on her."

Justin understood that he was responsible for his own attitude in regard to Sarah's sexual issues. He also realized that he did not have to let his disappointment control his actions toward her. He began to learn to be sympathetic to her past and to her present struggle. He also admitted to Sarah his imperfections in understanding and relating to her about her childhood sexual abuse, although he understood that he was not ultimately a failure for this lack of compassion. Finally, he let his love for her help him to believe in her and encourage her in her hard work of facing the abuse.

Justin came to learn that while he could not change Sarah, he could definitely influence her. He exerted that influence by encouraging her to pursue counseling. He indicated that, at first, Sarah was reluctant to share all the details of her abuse with the counselor. She didn't want to dig back into the pain of those experiences, but the counselor assured her that this was necessary for genuine healing, and that for so many years she had covered her pain by pretense. That pain had never been extracted, the counselor said, and talking about it in the counseling setting was the best way to extract it and find genuine healing.

The counselor helped Sarah understand that her father was responsible for this act, and that as a child none of the responsibility was hers. With the counselor, she came to understand and work through her many conflicting emotions about her father. The counselor helped her apply reality-living principles. She recognized that her attitude toward her father was affecting her relationship with Justin. She could learn to accept responsibility for her attitude toward her father, and she realized her attitude and her emotions toward him did not need to control her actions in her marriage. Since her father was deceased, the counselor helped her symbolically confront him with what had happened, and release him to God who judges righteously. In so doing, Sarah found emotional relief and healing.

The counselor also helped Justin understand how to be supportive of Sarah as she sought inner healing and how to be patient with her as she developed a healthier perspective on sex. In Justin's own words: "Beginning with holding hands and progressing to warm hugs, we have moved down the road. I have tried not to push her and to be understanding when the progress sometimes seems slow. I now feel that we are genuinely beginning to express love to each other sexually. I believe that things will get better as we continue to learn and grow. I just wanted you to know that your seminar was the beginning of our healing."

Justin's letter is a clear reminder that indeed, love is the most powerful weapon for good in the world. Justin and Sarah's love for each other gave them the desire and stamina to overcome her abusive past. Justin's letter is just the kind of encouragement that keeps marriage enrichment leaders motivated.

I want to make several observations about the progress that Justin and Sarah made. First, progress came as this couple began to take sexual abuse seriously. Whitewashing the problem of childhood sexual abuse will never remove the distorted emotions.

Second, both partners must be willing to break the silence and talk to someone outside the marriage about the problem. Sarah had tried this several years earlier when she shared her history with Justin, and together they shared it with a pastor. But the process was frustrated when there was no follow-through.

> *True healing will require the help of a fellow human being who can hear the pain, empathize with the hurt, and offer understanding and guidance.*

Problems related to sexual abuse are seldom solved unless a couple reaches out for help, which leads me to the third observation: A trained counselor can have a key role. Few couples will find lasting answers to the fallout of sexual abuse without the help of a trained professional.

If childhood sexual abuse is a factor in your marriage, reading good books on the subject can get you started in the right direction, but true healing will require the help of a fellow human being who can hear the pain, empathize with the hurt, and offer understanding and guidance.

BRENT: COMING TO TERMS WITH THE PAST

Victims of sexual abuse are not limited to the female gender. Research is indicating that a growing number of young men also suffer sexual abuse as children. This abuse often affects these boys in three areas: psychological distress, substance abuse, and sexually related problems.[2]

Betsy had been married for six years when she came to my office for counseling. She was a beautiful young lady from a fine Southern home. Her parents were pillars in the community, and her life was a picture of success. At least that was the way it appeared. But in my office, her beautiful face was streaked with rivulets of tears.

"We've been married for six years," she said. "Everyone thinks that we have a perfect marriage. The fact is, my husband and I have never been sexually intimate in the six years of our marriage, and what hurts me the most is that it doesn't seem to matter to him. I read books that talk about the male sex drive, but I don't see it in my husband. Brent seems to have no interest at all. For a while it didn't bother me because I thought it would change, but now I don't think it will.

"I want to have intimacy in my marriage, and I don't want to leave Brent, but I don't know what to do. We've talked about it a few times, and he's told me not to worry about it, but I do worry about it. It's just not right. Something is wrong, and I don't know what to do about it."

> *"It never went beyond hugging and kissing, and eventually even that stopped."*

In coming to me, Betsy was taking the first step in reality living. She was going against her emotions of fear in reaching out for help. I commended her for taking this brave step and assured her that I would help her take additional steps in her efforts to be an agent of positive change in her marriage. During our ensuing dialogue, she recounted her relationship with Brent before marriage.

"We met only a year before we got married. He is the only man I ever really loved. Before marriage, I didn't see anything that caused me to question his sexuality. He hugged and kissed me with passion. We never had sexual intercourse, and I was grateful that he never pushed me in this way. It was one of the things that I respected about him."

"After marriage, did he continue to kiss and hug you?" I asked.

"Yes, for a while. But we never had intercourse. He always said, 'Let's take it slow.' That was fine with me at first, but it never went beyond hugging and kissing, and eventually even that stopped. In other ways, Dr. Chapman, Brent is a wonderful husband. He's a hard worker; he treats me with kindness and respect; we enjoy doing things together. We really have a good marriage except for this one area."

"After six years of marriage," I said, "I think it's rather obvious that this problem is not going to take care of itself, and I think you are wise to be reaching out for help. However, we can't get very far without Brent's cooperation. I want to suggest that you go home and, within the next two or three days, tell Brent that you've been thinking a lot about your marriage and that in many ways he is the most wonderful husband you could imagine. Give him positive affirmation for his good qualities but also tell him that you are very disappointed in the sexual part of your marriage, that you have decided you are going for counseling to try to find out how you can cope with the situation, and that you would like to invite him to go with you."

"He won't go," she blurted out. "I've asked him before. I know he won't go for counseling."

"I'm sure you are right, but he can't keep you from going. What you are doing is informing Brent of the steps that you are taking.

He can never say that you went behind his back. You are telling him your motivation up front. You are probably right that he will not be willing to come with you. At any rate, call my office and make another appointment. Let Brent know when you are seeing me, and again invite him to go with you. If he is still unwilling, then you come alone. Now that he knows you have come to see me, it will give me the freedom to call him after our next session and let him know that you have shared with me something of the problem in your marriage. I can assure Brent that you seem to be sincere in your efforts of wanting to deal with the problem, but that I cannot help you without at least having one session with him to find out his perspective on the problem. Most of the time, when I call husbands in this situation, they will agree to come in for at least one session."

She agreed to our strategy. Brent was unwilling to come with her, but he did come to see me alone. In the first session, he poured out his story of sexual abuse as a child by a favorite uncle and later by a cousin. This drew him into homosexual relationships with several different partners, he explained. In college, he had both homosexual and heterosexual relationships. In fact, he became obsessed with sex and flunked out of college after his second year. Shortly thereafter, he had a religious conversion. Brent's overt sexual behavior changed almost instantly, but his internal fascination with sex led him to obsessive masturbation.

When he met Betsy at church, he was elated to think that a girl of her stature and purity would be interested in him. Of course, she knew nothing of his past sexual lifestyle, and he was not about to tell her for fear that he would lose her. In building his relationship with Betsy before they were married, Brent became emotionally revolted by his own earlier sexual history and wished that he were as pure as she. Sex became almost a devil to him, and he came to hate his own sexuality. In fighting this personal, emotional warfare against his past failures, he became impotent.

This impotence restrained his temptation to be sexually active with Betsy before marriage, but after marriage it also rendered him incapable of having a normal sexual relationship with her. He had hoped that the problem would soon go away and that Betsy would never have to know of his struggle. The problem had not gone away, however, and in coming to see me, Brent was sharing his story for the first time.

HONESTY AND HEALING

Because of his openness, I knew that Brent was on the road to recovery. It often takes numerous counseling sessions for a man to reveal what he had revealed to me in our first session. I told him how grateful I was that he had chosen to see me and how encouraged I was that he was so open. I assured him that this was the first step toward healing. I told him that I thought his wife would be supportive and that I believed, with counseling, they could solve this problem.

I asked Brent if he would be willing to come with Betsy the next time and in my presence share with her something of what he had shared with me. He said that he would but that it would be the hardest thing that he had ever done in his life. "That's probably true," I said. "And one of the best things you've ever done in your life." I later called Betsy and asked if I could see her briefly the day before our counseling session together. She agreed. I tried to prepare her for what she was going to hear and told her how happy I was that her husband had chosen to share these things with me and was now willing to share them with her. I did not reveal the content of what Brent would tell her, but I did tell Betsy that what she would hear would make her very sad and perhaps spark anger and other emotions inside of her.

I knew that Betsy had a strong faith, and I suggested that she ask God to give her the ability to accept the truth and the strength to work through the problems. I encouraged her to apply reality-living principles. While Brent's revelation might raise negative emotions within her, I reminded her that she did not have to let those emotions control her actions or her attitude toward him. She could still encourage and support Brent. I also reminded her that she could not change him, but that she could certainly influence him. In fact, I told her that I felt she was a key element in Brent's being willing to be open with me and that I believed with her support, he would take the necessary steps to find healing. I reminded her to hang on to the love she felt for him throughout this sometimes-difficult process of healing. I knew that her love would be the most powerful weapon for good in this situation.

With great strength but not without fear, he confronted those who had abused him.

The next session went as I had hoped. Brent was open; he told his wife about his past homosexual (and heterosexual) involvement. He expressed deep guilt, and he told her that if she could no longer accept him, he would understand. Betsy said with tears, "I am very disappointed, but I love you. And I will stick with you, and with God's help, we will find an answer to this problem." She did. And they did.

In the following weeks, I counseled with Brent weekly. We walked through his past. With great strength but not without fear, he confronted those who had originally abused him. They did what typically happens—denied that they had done anything wrong. But in confronting them, Brent assured his own healing. Releasing the abusers to God, he also released his resentment and recognized that in spite of what they had done to him as a child, he could now, as an adult, find healing.

Brent learned that his emotions toward his abusers did not need to control his actions. He realized that he alone was responsible for his attitude toward the abuse and that he could choose not to let it control his actions and attitudes toward sex within his marriage. He also realized that he could not change his abusers, although he did hope to influence them by confronting them. He was able to admit his imperfections about his own sexual choices before he met Betsy, but he also understood that those choices did not mean he was a complete failure.

After the first two sessions with Brent, I met again with Betsy and told her that I thought that within the next few weeks, her husband would begin to reach out to her with physical touch. I encouraged her to be responsive to his initiatives but not to push anything, to let him move at his own pace. Within three weeks, he was indeed reaching out to hold hands as they watched television together. And a week later, he embraced her and kissed her passionately. Within three months, the impotency was gone. At that juncture, I began marriage counseling with them for several sessions, helping them look at their entire relationship and develop positive ways of communicating with each other.

Once the sexual barrier was overcome, they progressed rapidly. For several years now, they have had what they both consider to be a normal sex life. Betsy's only regret is that she did not reach out for help much sooner.

As is often the case, Betsy, a supportive spouse, initiated the process, which eventually led Brent, a victim of childhood sexual abuse, to get help. A supportive spouse is a great asset on this journey toward healing from childhood sexual abuse. Love is indeed the most powerful weapon for good in the world.

Childhood sexual abuse greatly impacts every victim. It distorts the victim's emotions and thoughts related to sexuality. These distortions will differ with each victim depending on unique personality differences, but the answer lies in facing the issue squarely and getting help.

If you are a victim of childhood sexual abuse, you can learn to act on reality-living principles. You can acknowledge your own failures without taking on the responsibility for the original abuse. You can also come to recognize that your thinking and emotions are distorted and then learn to go against your feelings of fear and shame and reach out to find help.

WHEN YOUR HUSBAND
SEXUALLY ABUSES YOUR CHILDREN

Before we leave the subject of sexual abuse, I want to tell you about Robbie, who attended one of my seminars in Birmingham. Tears flowed freely as she said, "I discovered recently that my husband has sexually abused both of our daughters. One is now sixteen and the other is eighteen. Apparently this has gone on for several years, but I didn't know it until about a month ago. My older daughter finally went for counseling on her college campus; that's what brought it all out. Then she talked with my younger daughter and found out that the same thing had been happening to her. As soon as I heard it, I took my daughter and went to live with my mother. Right now, I hate my husband, Gene, and never want to see him again."

I found out that she had talked with Gene only once since she left. He told her that he knew what he did was wrong and that he regretted it and that he was sincerely sorry, and he promised her that if she would come back, he would make certain that it would never happen again. Robbie said, "Right now, I am so confused I don't know what to do."

I am not usually this dogmatic, but I said to Robbie, "I can tell you what to do. Continue to live with your mother. Help both of your daughters find a counselor who has experience in helping victims of sexual abuse. Be willing to go with your daughters as the counselor requests." The reason I emphasized this is that many daughters have resentment toward their mother for allowing this to happen. In Robbie's case, she may not have known what was going on, but I can almost guarantee that in their minds, they feel she is somewhat responsible.

If the daughters each deal honestly with the counselor and their mother, there can be healing, and the girls can rise above the scars of childhood sexual abuse. Dealing with the issues thoroughly at this stage in their lives is far better than glossing over the problem and hoping that the scars of abuse will not show up in their marriages. Unless there is genuine deep healing the abuse will most certainly have a detrimental effect on their future relationships.

I continued talking with Robbie: "As for Gene, do not let him talk you into coming back home. You need time to process your own hurt as do your daughters." I said this because research has shown that a father who has abused multiple children over a long period of time will not change his behavior simply because someone catches him.[3] He may cry, he may express sorrow, he may make promises, but none of these can be taken at face value. His actions will speak louder than his words.

"If Gene is sincere about dealing with his sexual abuse, then he will get his own counselor and begin the long road of personal healing. He will also give you and your daughter financial assistance while you are living with your mother, and he will do the same for your daughter who is in college. If he tries to manipulate you into coming back by with-holding finances, you will know that he is not sincere."

"Your daughters should never be left alone with their father. If in the counseling process they can come together with the counselor to confront, hear their father's confession, and choose to forgive, that can be a part of the healing process. But forgiveness does not rebuild trust nor restore a close relationship. The same is true in your relationship with Gene. If he gets extensive counseling and you do the same, the day may come when you can have a 'repent and forgive' session with a counselor. However, this does not necessarily lead to the reconciliation of your marriage."

I don't know what happened to Robbie, her husband, or her daughters. That was my last

Religious teachings must never be used to rush a victim to premature and surface forgiveness, and religious conversion must never be used as a quick solution to an abuser's problem.

contact with her. I do know that they each needed counseling and time to process their deep hurt. There is life after sexual abuse, but time alone does not heal pain. Each individual must deal openly, honestly, and thoroughly with his or her experience.

If this pattern of abuse is happening to a child or other family member, do as Robbie did and remove yourself and your loved ones from the situation as soon as possible and get some help.

The spiritual dimension of healing is very important. The acknowledging of moral boundaries and accepting responsibility for breaking these boundaries form an important part of the healing process. Admitting wrongdoing, giving and receiving forgiveness, and finding peace with God also are important in healing such relationships. However, religious teachings must never be used to rush a victim to premature and surface forgiveness, and religious conversion must never be used as a quick solution to an abuser's problem. Conversion sets in motion positive changes, but it does not solve all problems immediately. Religious conversion can chart the course for healing, but abusers and victims still have to make the journey a day at a time.

If you have experienced sexual abuse or live with a spouse who has, it is my sincere desire that this chapter may serve as the spark to get you started on the road toward healing.

Your situation may not exactly parallel the three that we have examined in this chapter, but I trust you will see some common threads that run through all the stories of sexual abuse victims and their subsequent marriages. Time alone does not heal the results of sexual abuse. Breaking the barriers of denial, guilt, shame, anger, and fear must precede healing.

All of this begins with a single step. Someone must reach out for help. Usually, it will be the spouse of the abused victim.[4] If you are such a spouse, know that you can be the agent of positive change in your marriage by helping your spouse get the help he or she needs in order to find inner healing from childhood sexual abuse and, in time, marital healing.

FOR FURTHER HELP

- celebraterecovery.com: Founded by Rick Warren and Saddleback Church, this is a national network of faith-based recovery groups seeking to help those struggling with a broad variety of issues, including but not limited to addictions
- Dan B. Allender, PhD, *The Wounded Heart: Hope for Adult Victims of Childhood Sexual Abuse* (Colorado Springs: NavPress, 2008).

PART 4

Disconnected
Spouses

11

The Uncommunicative Spouse

K atelyn was a free-spirited, laughing, loving, and caring person.

In her office, the other women in her department tried to take their break when Katelyn was on break because they enjoyed her positive spirit. But in my office, she was not laughing. Tears long held inside were now cascading down her normally cheerful face. "Chris won't talk to me," she said. "I mean, he really won't talk to me. It's tearing me up inside.

"I'm usually a happy person," she continued. "I can adapt and get along with almost anyone, but I don't know what to do when Chris won't talk to me. I ask him what's wrong, and he sits there in silence as though I said nothing. Last night I told him, 'Chris, we have got to talk. We can't go on like this.' He got up and left the room."

"How long has this been going on?" I inquired.

"It started last Sunday night when I told him that I wanted to spend the weekend at the beach with two of the women I work with. One of their parents owns a place at the beach; it wouldn't cost us anything. It would be a good chance for us to spend some time together and relax. Chris went ballistic. He told me that, as a married woman, I had no right going to the beach with girlfriends. He said that if I were going to the beach, we needed to go together. He said, 'Why would you even want to go to the beach with girls from work? Is there something going on that I don't know about?'

"Dr. Chapman, I've never been unfaithful to Chris. I don't even have such thoughts. Why does he accuse me of that? I told him he was being immature and that he had no right to tell me that I couldn't go to the beach. After all, he spends most Saturdays playing golf.

"We're not leaving until Friday after work, and I'll be home Sunday night. He'll hardly even miss me. We went to bed angry that night and since then, Chris has not said a word to me. That was a week ago last night."

"Has he ever been silent like this before?" I asked.

"Two or three times," she said. "But usually just for a day or maybe two. Never this long."

"Does he talk when you are not having conflicts like this?" I asked.

"Well, he doesn't talk as much as I do," Katelyn said. "He's kind of quiet, but he does talk. I don't have any complaints normally. But his silence is driving me crazy."

"What are you feeling toward Chris right now?" I asked.

"I don't understand him," she said. "I feel that he is trying to control my life. I don't know why he would do that. I don't try to control him. Last fall, he went fishing for a week with his friends. I didn't get bent out of shape. That was fine with me. I think he needs some time with his friends, but I need time with my friends also. Why would he get so upset about this and not talk?"

I asked if she thought Chris would come see me.

"I don't think so, Dr. Chapman. He thinks that talking to other people about your problems is a sign of weakness. He has always said that he can solve his own problems." Did Chris know that his wife had come in for counseling? "No, and if he did he would be upset," she said.

HIS NEED FOR LOVE, HER NEED FOR FREEDOM

Katelyn and Chris had been married only about a year. They had attended the marriage preparation classes that I had taught, so I knew a little bit about Chris's personality. So I said to Katelyn, "It may be necessary later on for me to talk to Chris, but let's try something first. Much behavior in marriage is motivated by unmet emotional needs. For example, you came to my office today because of unmet needs in your own life. You want to have an intimate, open, caring, loving relationship with Chris; and right now, you don't have that. All of us need to feel loved, but at the moment, you don't feel that he's loving you. Rather, you feel that he is trying to control your behavior.

"Another need that all of us have is the need for freedom. Chris's efforts to keep you from going to the beach are removing your sense of freedom; thus, two of your deepest emotional needs are not being met—the need for freedom and the need for love."

Katelyn was nodding, and I continued. "Now, Chris is also a person who has emotional needs. His behavior can also be explained in terms of unmet needs. He has the need to be loved by you, to feel that he is number one in your life. My guess is that he does not feel that at the moment. He may feel that the women with whom you are going to the beach are more important to you than he is, that you love them more than you love him. Thus, one of his fundamental emotional needs is unmet at the moment—the need for love."

I suggested his silent treatment was his way of telling her, "This is a serious problem." His silence could also be an effort to manipulate Katelyn into agreeing not to go to the beach. "He may have used this approach with his parents during his childhood or teenage years," I said. "Perhaps his parents caved in to his desires when he gave them the silent treatment."

"I saw that twice when we were dating," she replied. "His mother didn't like his silence, and she ended up doing what he wanted."

"Then maybe we've discovered a learned behavior pattern in Chris's life that needs to be changed. The ideal," I said, "is to find a way where you can meet his need for emotional love and at the same time maintain your own freedom."

Then I asked her if she knew her husband's primary love language. We had discussed the five love languages during the premarital classes, and Katelyn felt confident Chris's was physical touch. So I asked her to think back over the last month. "Now I want you to answer this question: 'How effective have I been in speaking Chris's primary love language over the past four weeks?'"

Katelyn thought for a moment and said, "Dr. Chapman, we've been so busy that I have to admit I haven't spoken his language very much in the last month. His love tank is probably empty so he's threatened by my going to the beach. He feels unloved and like I'm deserting him." (That's the moment of insight that counselors wait for—when people see their situation clearly and understand what they need to do.)

WHAT KATELYN SAID TO CHRIS

Then I suggested the following: "What if you go home and say to Chris something like this: 'Chris, I want you to know that I love you very much. I have been thinking about us a lot since our argument on Sunday night, and I have realized that I have not spoken your primary love language very well in the last few weeks. It's not because I don't want to; it's because I've been so busy I just haven't taken time to be with you and express my love to you. I think that your opposition to my going to the beach is largely because I have not filled your love tank. I thought at first that you were trying to control my life, but I really don't believe that's true.

"'I know that I give you freedom to go golfing with your friends, and I believe that you want to give me freedom to be with my friends. I also want you to know that your silence this week and unwillingness to talk with me has caused me great pain and hurt because it communicates to me that you don't love me. I'm going to request that you never do this again because it hurts me so deeply, and I can tell you that I will never let you control my behavior by such silence.

"'I'm going to the beach next month with my friends, but we have three weeks before that weekend. I want to show you my love. I want to hold you and kiss you and hug you and be sexually intimate with you. Hey, we can have sex every day between now and then if you want.'" (Kate caught my humor, and she was smiling now.)

I continued: "'Chris, I love you, and I'm so sorry that we wasted this week in our lives. Now, how about a kiss and a hug for starters?'

"If Chris doesn't respond to this approach, then I want you to tell him that you are going to call me and come in for an appointment, that you are not going on with the silent treatment. Once you've called me and set the appointment, you invite him to come with you. If he won't come, you come alone. Now he has the knowledge that you've seen me, and the next day, I will call him and ask him to come in and talk with me about the situation. I think he will come because I think he respects me." She nodded again.

"I think he'd come, Dr. Chapman, but I want to try the other approach first."

"Good," I said. "But be assured that I'm willing to call Chris, and I want to say to you that you cannot afford to allow the silence to continue. It's not natural, and it's not a healthy way for him to be responding to his unmet need for love. You must not allow this pattern to get established in your relationship."

Two weeks later, I saw Katelyn at a public gathering, talking with some friends. She came over, smiled and said, "It worked. He started talking that same night. He told me how sorry he was that he had treated me so badly. He realized that was not a healthy way for him to respond, and he said he hoped that he would not do that again. I think I've got his love tank full, Dr. Chapman. I'm going to the beach next weekend. Chris has agreed and feels good about it."

"Have a great time," I said. I walked away with the confidence that Chris and Katelyn had learned a great deal about themselves and each other through their painful experience with the silent treatment.

One of the encouraging things about the couple's story is that Katelyn took positive action early in the marriage to deal with a silent partner. She put reality living principles to work. She realized that she was responsible for her own attitude and that her attitude affected her actions toward him. She understood that her emotions of frustration with Chris did not need to control her actions toward him. She could take positive steps to resolve this issue with her husband despite any negative feelings toward him, knowing that her actions could influence him. She admitted to herself and to Chris that she had not been speaking his love language, although this did not mean she had completely failed in her marriage. Finally, she allowed love to do its powerful work.

This was the first time Chris had ever treated her with silence for an extended period. She came for help and gained insight, understanding, and a strategy for dealing with the problem. Solving such problems early in marriage is always the ideal. Unfortunately, many couples have allowed the silent treatment to get entrenched in their relationship over many years of marriage.

NOT JUST A "MALE THING"

I am often asked at my marriage seminars if it is a male thing not to talk. While it is true that many men talk less than their wives, it is not true that men are the only non-communicating spouses.

I first met Andy in Seattle, the city of eternal rain. He had on a T-shirt that said, "You Can Tell When It's Summer in Seattle . . . The Rain Is Warmer." I laughed at his T-shirt, but I did not laugh at his story.

"Dr. Chapman, we've been married for five years now, and we've had a fairly good marriage. The only real problem is that Liz keeps everything inside and will not share with me her thoughts and feelings, especially if they're negative. I think it's because she grew up in a home where her thoughts and emotions were never welcomed. If she shared a negative emotion, she got a lecture on why she shouldn't feel that way. If she shared her thoughts and they were different from her father's, he told her that she was wrong. So she developed a pattern of holding her thoughts and feelings inside.

"I have tried to tell her that I'm not her dad. I consider myself a good listener. I don't get angry and scream at her. I've even taken some courses at church as a lay counselor, and I would like to help her open up. But it's really hard."

"Old patterns are hard to break," I said, "but I think you are moving in the right direction. She needs the assurance that you are there to listen, not to condemn." I asked if Liz was with him at the seminar.

"Yes," he said. "I'm really glad that she was willing to come."

"I'd like to meet her at the next break if possible," I said.

When I saw Liz, I shared with her the gist of what Andy had told me, to which she responded, "Dr. Chapman, I wish I could open up to Andy. I really want to. I know it's important not only for him but also for me. But I feel when I share negative feelings and thoughts it makes me a bad person. I shouldn't have negative feelings, and I shouldn't think negative thoughts."

"What are the feelings that you have most difficulty sharing?" I asked.

"Anger is one," she said. "I wish I didn't get angry. Depression is another. Sometimes I feel so depressed; I hate myself when I feel that way."

I knew that she was active in her local church because Andy had told me, so I said to her, "Did you know that Jesus often felt angry and that Jesus also felt depressed?" Liz looked shocked and said, "Really?"

"Yes," I said, "Anger and depression are common human feelings. They certainly do not mean that you are a bad person. Anger arises inside when you perceive that you or someone else has been treated unfairly. Anger reveals your concern for righteousness and justice. Anger is not wrong. The Bible says of God that He "is angry with the wicked every day."[1] Jesus felt depressed hours before He went to the cross, but He did not allow His depression to control His behavior.[2] Negative emotions are not sinful," I said. "They simply reveal that we are humans and that when we encounter certain situations in life, we feel depressed or sad.

"The important thing is that you do not allow your negative emotions to lead you to wrongful behavior. Sharing these emotions with Andy or anyone is a positive part of the process of not allowing them to control your behavior.

"We process negative emotions by sharing them with a trusted friend. Emotions come and go. When we talk about them, they tend to go. When we hold them inside, they tend to stay."

WRITING DOWN YOUR FEELINGS

I suggested to Liz what I've suggested to many people through the years.

"If you find it difficult to break the barrier of silence, try writing your thoughts and feelings in a letter to your spouse. Many times it is easier to write than it is to speak of such feelings. But as you become comfortable writing the letters and your spouse reads them with understanding and comfort and encouragement, you will eventually learn to verbalize your feelings and thoughts. Writing can be a big step in the process of learning how to communicate openly with your inner self." Liz assured me that she would try this because she knew that it was important in her relationship with Andy.

Like Katelyn, Liz realized that she was responsible for her own attitude about emotions, especially negative emotions. She realized how much this was affecting her behavior in her marriage and hurting Andy. She admitted her imperfections in this area while also realizing that this did not mean she was a failure in her marriage. Finally, she allowed the power of her love for Andy to help her begin to face her emotions and share them with him through writing.

Six months later, I got an email from Andy telling me how thankful he was for my comments to her. She had indeed started writing him letters almost immediately after the seminar, and now she was able to share verbally her thoughts and feelings with him.

I responded to Andy that one of the reasons Liz was able to break this pattern of silence in her life was because he had demonstrated to her by words and actions the art of empathetic listening. Had he condemned her thoughts and feelings or gotten angry with her, she would have stopped the flow of words immediately. He too sought not to change his wife but rather to influence her. He chose to be an agent of positive change and let his love for her do its powerful work through listening.

LOU RETREATS TO THE DEN

The reality is that many spouses have retreated to the den of silence because they fear their spouse's response.

I well remember the husband who said to me, "She's right. I don't talk. When I come home, I go into the den, watch TV, go online, or read. And when my wife asks me to talk, I just keep on with what I'm doing. Because every time I share a thought or an idea, she pounces on it and tells me why I shouldn't think that way. If I comment on something in the news she will always take the opposite side. If I tell her about something that happened during my day and give my opinion on it, she always has a different opinion.

"This has gone on ever since we got married. So I've decided it's safer not to talk. I can't take her constant disagreement with everything I say."

When I talked to this man's wife, Karla, her perspective was that her husband was dogmatic and opinionated and that most of the time his opinions were wrong and she was trying to help him see another perspective. She couldn't understand why he got so defensive when she disagreed with his ideas. She took that as immaturity and told him so. Lou had stopped talking for fear that any comment he made would provoke what he considered to be an attack from Karla.

Later, as Lou and I talked further, I discovered that in childhood, he was never allowed to express his ideas. Whenever Lou did share an idea, his father was quick to correct him.

Now as an adult, he had become a widely read person and felt that he had a rather good perspective on what was going on in the world. He prided himself in this knowledge. This had been his way of building his own self-esteem, seeking to overcome the negative messages he received from his father. When his wife disagreed with his ideas, it struck deeply at his self-esteem. That is why Lou became defensive, and that is why he eventually stopped talking.

A QUESTION, NOT A COMMENT

It took awhile, but eventually we discovered that if Karla would frame her thoughts in the form of a question rather than a comment, Lou could receive it with less defensiveness. "What do you think about this perspective?" was easier for him to receive than for his wife to state an opposing view.

After considerable counseling, Lou came to recognize that Karla's expressions of her ideas, though different from his, were not in fact designed to condemn him. He came to understand that people can have different ideas and still like each other, and that when we give people the freedom to disagree with us, we give them the freedom to be human.

People can have different ideas and still like each other.

Lou was willing to talk again when he finally concluded that his wife was not against him. She just wanted the freedom to be a person and express her ideas even if they were different from his ideas.

Lou realized that he was responsible for his own attitude about talking to his wife. He now understood how that attitude had developed and could see how it was affecting his marriage. He chose not to let his negative emotions in this area affect the way he perceived his wife's comments to him. When admitting that he was imperfect in this area, he understood that he was not a complete failure in his marriage. Rather, he understood that because of his love for Karla, he was willing to work on this area of imperfection.

UNMET NEEDS

There are many reasons why some spouses become uncommunicative. Their unwillingness to share verbally finds its root in what is going on inside of them. Often it is unmet needs in the marital relationship that have sparked resentment in the spirit of the silent spouse. His silence is a way of expressing this resentment. It is her way of saying, "I don't like you so I will treat you as a nonperson."

I don't mean that the silent partner is consciously thinking these thoughts; I mean these are the inner emotional reasons why he or she is not talking. If you can discover the emotions inside your uncommunicative spouse and the factors that give rise to these emotions, you will be well on your way to helping your spouse to break his or her silence.

The spouse who seeks to be an agent of positive change in his or her marriage would do well to ask this question: "Does my spouse have an unmet emotional need that may be causing him to resent me?"

A positive answer to one of these questions may uncover your spouse's unmet needs and thus the source of his or her silence. Your challenge will be to find a way to help your spouse meet that emotional need and at the same time maintain your own integrity and get your own emotional needs met.

DO YOU SILENCE YOUR SPOUSE?

Another way to become an agent for change is to ask yourself: Does my communication pattern make it difficult for my spouse to talk? Negative communication patterns can silence a spouse. The solution is to change those patterns.

Here are some questions you can ask yourself to determine whether your conversations with your spouse are negative. Answer each one honestly with a yes or a no.

- Do I often come across as complaining?
- When my spouse talks, do I cut him off and give my responses?
- Do I force the issue of communication with my spouse, even in those times when she needs to be alone?
- Do I broadcast our private conversations to others?
- Do I openly share my own needs and desires as demands?
- When my spouse shares an opinion that differs from mine, am I quick to "set him straight"?

If you can answer yes to any of these questions, it may be time for you to change a negative communication pattern. Changing these patterns may be difficult, but it is the way toward loosening the tongue of your uncommunicative spouse.

One of the best ways to do this is to develop the art of listening. If you exhibit the sincere desire to understand your spouse through listening, you will enhance the climate of open communication. There are many ways you can communicate "I care about what you say" just by listening. Give your spouse your undivided attention when he or she is talking; maintain eye contact when possible; turn off the TV; lay down the book (or Facebook), and give your mate your focused attention. All these actions communicate, "Your words matter to me."

To receive your spouse's ideas as information rather than as an opinion that you must correct creates an atmosphere of acceptance. This doesn't mean that you agree with all of those ideas; it simply means that you give your spouse the freedom to hold those ideas.

Learning to control your anger and to hear your spouse out also enhances communication. Loud, angry outbursts almost always stop the flow of communication. Practice "reflective listening," reflecting back your spouse's words in your own words. "Are you saying . . ." and "What I hear you saying is . . ." are phrases that help your spouse continue to clarify what he/she is saying. At times, indicate your understanding of the message: "I think I understand . . . I see what you're saying . . . That makes a lot of sense." Such statements tend to keep your spouse talking. All of us are more likely to communicate our inner thoughts and feelings if we believe that someone genuinely wants to hear what we want to say and will not condemn us.

Another way to become an agent of positive change with an uncommunicative spouse would be to read or attend a course at a local college or church on the art of communication. If your spouse would join you in such a course or in reading a book, so much the better. But don't wait for him or her to join you. Take the initiative; go against your feelings if you must, but do something positive to enhance your own understanding of why people do not communicate.

Obviously, if whatever you have tried in the past to help your spouse communicate has not worked, then it's time to take a new approach. Put the principles of reality living to work in your marriage.

12

The Unfaithful Spouse

"I plight thee my troth" was the old-style way of saying it. Most modern ceremonies include the words "I pledge you my faithfulness."

Examine most contemporary and historic marriage ceremonies, and you will find the idea of sexual faithfulness repeated more than once. When couples come to the marriage altar, they understand that they are committing themselves to be involved sexually with each other, and that this means that they will not be involved sexually with anyone else as long as they are married to each other.

Who of us would honestly say, "If my spouse desires to have sexual relations with someone else, it is perfectly fine with me"? Such a statement usually is made only by someone whose marriage has already died and/or someone who is already involved

> *Who among us would say, "If my spouse desires to have sexual relations with someone else, it is perfectly fine with me"?*

with someone else and is subconsciously trying to find a way to end the marriage.

Yes, we care about sexual fidelity in marriage. It is not simply a moral or religious concern, although most religions do call for sexual fidelity in marriage. Our concern for sexual faithfulness in marriage is rooted in our humanity. It has to do with integrity and character. It is tied to our emotional need for love. It grows out of a person's desire for an exclusive relationship with someone who will not only value her above all others, but also someone to whom she can be fully and totally committed. It is this inner sense of commitment that gives stability to marriage. Sexual infidelity destroys this security and leaves in its wake fear, doubt, distrust, and a sense of betrayal.

Perhaps nothing is more painful to an individual and more destructive to a marriage than discovering that your spouse has been sexually unfaithful to you. Infidelity strikes at the heart of marital unity.

There are different kinds and levels of sexual involvement outside of marriage. The so-called one-night stand is the brief, spur-of-the-moment sexual liaison, which is essentially sex without relationship. The long-term affair, on the other hand, begins with an emotional involvement that leads eventually to sexual involvement. Another form of involvement has the spouse finding multiple sexual partners outside the marriage. There are also those who have homosexual or lesbian relationships outside the marriage. Though each of these is somewhat different, they all are devastating to marital intimacy.

RAPHAEL: "WILL IT HAPPEN AGAIN?"

If you discover that your spouse has been sexually unfaithful, or if he or she reveals such information to you, you will likely experience a cascade of various emotions. Hurt, anger, bitterness, the sense of being betrayed, shame, and perhaps some measure of guilt may all rush to the surface.

Raphael was feeling this way. I met him in beautiful sunny southern California. He was the picture of health, and I supposed that his bronze skin and handsome physique caught the eyes of many women. But Raphael was not a womanizer. He was devoted to his wife, Joanna, to whom he had been married for fifteen years. They met in college. The early years of their marriage had been exciting for both of them, but more recently he felt a growing distance developing between them. He tried to discuss his feelings with Joanna, but she didn't want to talk about it until one day when she finally let the words rush out: "I was involved with a man at work, and we have been lovers for the past two years."

Joanna said that she was sorry and didn't want to hurt him— that was why she hadn't told him before. And while the other man had now left the state and declared the relationship finished, Raphael's wife felt heartbroken. She was still emotionally bonded to the man from work. At times, she felt extremely guilty for what she had done. Raphael had been a good husband. At other times, she knew that she would do it again given the same circumstances. Even now, if her lover called, she would probably get on the first plane to New York.

Raphael was not totally surprised by Joanna's confession. He knew that things had not been right between them for some time. Still, he felt crushed at the thought of her being in the arms of another man. He felt anger toward the other man and pity for Joanna that she had allowed herself to be pulled into such a relationship. He loved Joanna and hoped that they could rebuild their marriage, but he was plagued by the reality that this was not the first time she had been involved with someone else. Early in their marriage, she had developed an emotional attachment to a man she met playing tennis. She had not gotten sexually involved at that time. At least, she had not shared that with Raphael. But he wondered. He also wondered if there had been other relationships along the way.

The question that plagued him most was: "Will it happen again?" The disappointment, hurt, anger, and worry were overwhelming at times. He had fleeting thoughts of suicide and lingering thoughts of killing the other man. He loved Joanna in spite of all that had happened, but he did not know if he could really trust her again.

Three years after I first met Raphael, I had an extended conversation in which he shared with me what had happened after Joanna revealed her unfaithfulness to him. What he shared is a rather classic example of a man who followed the principles of reality living in responding to his wife's sexual unfaithfulness. In the rest of this chapter, I want to share with you Raphael's story and clarify the value of handling this kind of crisis in a responsible manner.

Wrestling the myths

First, let me remind you of the four myths that you must reject if you are going to practice reality living.

Myth Number One: My environment determines my state of mind.

Myth Number Two: People cannot change.

Myth Number Three: In a desperate marriage, I have only two options—resigning myself to a life of misery or getting out of the marriage.

Myth Number Four: Some situations are hopeless—and my situation is one of these.

Raphael had to wrestle with each of these myths. Any one of them could have deterred him from taking positive action. Immediately following Joanna's disclosure, Raphael's most intense emotion was hurt and disappointment. He wept for a full thirty minutes after she finished her revelation. He said nothing; he was too overwhelmed with grief. Then there was the surge of anger, first toward the other man and later toward her. Then followed depression, that sense of hopelessness; that nothing could be done to repair the damage, that their marriage was forever lost.

All of these emotions and others rolled in and out of Raphael's life over the first week. He took no strong action, he made no angry speeches to Joanna; he found himself withdrawing from her, oversleeping in the mornings, and by the end of the first week, decided to take a day off from work and spend some time alone.

It was during this day that Raphael realized he had an option: He could cave in to his emotions and become an angry, bitter, depressed man for the rest of his life; or, despite the painful feelings, he could choose to have a positive attitude and work to make a better future—with or without Joanna. He didn't know what direction she would go ultimately, but he knew in his heart that he owed it to himself, his parents, and his friends to think the best and to work toward positive goals.

Over the next couple of weeks, he wrestled with myths number two, three, and four. *People can't change*, he thought. *If Joanna has been emotionally involved with two men, sexually involved with at least one in our fifteen years of marriage, what assurance do I have that she will not repeat this pattern three years from now?* After all, behavioral patterns are hard to change, especially when they involve emotions and the sexual areas of life. He wondered if he had been deficient somehow in his efforts to be a good husband and had pushed Joanna to become involved with someone else, and, if so, he wondered if he could change. He knew that he could not resign himself to a life of misery if her affairs continued in the future. It was simply not something he was willing to live with.

> *Maybe his situation with Joanna was hopeless, but in his heart he really didn't believe that.*

He thought long and hard about the option of divorce—one option promoted by myth number three. In some ways, he found the idea appealing. If she liked another man, then let her have another man; he would walk his own way. He would build his own happiness, and Joanna would one day regret that she had walked away from him. But Raphael also knew that although divorce would let him walk away from a problem, ultimately it would create other problems. He knew that such action would not only affect him and Joanna but also his parents, her parents, and all the extended family who had looked up to them as an ideal couple.

Myth number four pounded hard on his mind: Some situations are hopeless—and my situation is one of these. *Am I knocking my head against the wall? Will things ever be different? If they won't, then wouldn't it be better to get out now rather than wasting years following an impossible dream?*

All of these myths tugged tenaciously at the back of his mind, but at the end of two or three weeks he said no to all of them. He knew others who had fought for their marriages and succeeded. People do change, and perhaps he and Joanna could both make the necessary changes to affect a good marriage. He decided that divorce was not an acceptable option, at least not without making every effort at reconciliation. Why give up now? If it came to divorce, why not make that the last option rather than the first? Maybe his situation with Joanna was hopeless, but in his heart he really didn't believe that. Having wrestled with the myths and won, he was now ready to apply the principles of reality living.

DOING THE HARD WORK

Raphael recognized that he was responsible for his own attitude.

Although Joanna's actions had sparked strong emotions inside of him, he chose to respond to those emotions in a constructive manner. He knew that he could focus on either the negative or the positive. He could wallow in his own pain and eventually become a bitter man, or he could acknowledge his hurt and anger and choose to work his way through these, looking for answers rather than surrendering to the devastating blows of these emotions. With his positive attitude, he was now ready to take constructive action.

He asked a friend for the name of the counselor who had helped him when he was having a rough time in his marriage. The next day, Raphael called the counselor and made an appointment. He decided to ask Joanna if she wanted to go with him, and she agreed. Their appointment with the counselor was exactly six weeks to the day after Joanna revealed to Raphael her involvement with the man at work. She had lived in a somewhat depressed state during this time, taking some medication she received from the doctor to get to sleep at night. She was generally confused about her feelings and wasn't sure she had the energy to see a counselor, but she agreed to go. Thus began the long and detailed process of finding healing from the fallout of sexual unfaithfulness and rebuilding a marriage.

One of the insights that Raphael gained in counseling was that he could not change Joanna, but that his behavior did influence her emotions. Nothing Raphael could do would guarantee that she would remain faithful to him. But he also learned that building an intimate marriage with Joanna that met both their emotional needs for companionship would be the greatest deterrent against future unfaithfulness.

With the counselor, Raphael and Joanna began to excavate their own needs in their marital relationship and to examine the manner in which these needs had or had not been met in the past. They recognized that each of their needs was unique and that if they were to build an intimate marriage, they must both come to understand the other, respect their individual differences, and make genuine efforts to meet each other's needs.

It's not uncommon, as a couple tries to climb out of the wreckage of infidelity, that one or the other wants to end their counseling sessions. That's how Raphael felt. He thought the counselor and Joanna were putting undue blame on him for her sexual unfaithfulness, implying that if he had met her needs, she would not have become involved with another man. A part of him wanted to stop the counseling.

When he shared his thinking with the counselor and Joanna, the counselor assured him that it was all right to have those thoughts and feelings. "Those are typical emotional responses when a couple begins to deal realistically with their marriage.

You can leave the counseling process any time you want," she assured Raphael. But the therapist also affirmed another principle of reality living—that our emotions should not control our actions. She reminded Raphael that he could acknowledge his emotions and the direction in which they were pushing him, but then choose to walk in an opposite direction, believing the overall benefit of doing so would be positive. Raphael stayed in counseling, and the process of reconciliation progressed.

One of the most difficult parts of the counseling for Raphael was admitting that he had not been as successful in meeting Joanna's emotional needs as he had assumed. He discovered, for example, that she had felt left out of the decision-making process because he often made decisions without discussing them with her. She did not feel significant.

Raphael was a strong, confident, insightful businessman. He made decisions daily in the business and prided himself on being a good decision maker. When it came to decision-making in the marriage, he had always considered Joanna's needs and made his decisions with her in mind. In fact, she had been pleased with most of his decisions, but she still felt isolated and left out of the process. She viewed him more as a father who was making benevolent decisions for his child. She saw herself as a child rather than a partner whose ideas and feelings were welcome at the discussion table. This perception of Raphael as a father rather than a partner had been a part of what had motivated her to look elsewhere for intimacy.

Understanding and admitting these emotional dynamics was painful for Raphael. He found help in another reality-living principle: Admitting my imperfections does not mean that I am a failure. The counselor helped Raphael understand that his intentions had been positive; his method of decision-making had been loving and altruistic toward Joanna; but it had not served her emotional need for companionship. Admitting this did not mean that he had been a failure; it simply meant that there was a better way to make decisions, and this involved communication with Joanna. With the counselor, Raphael and Joanna negotiated the changes they would need to make in the decision-making process.

The counselor helped Raphael and Joanna make several other discoveries about changes they needed to make in their marriage. They began to learn how to tell each other their feelings, thoughts, and desires without condemning the other person. They began to learn how to make requests rather than demands. They began to learn the joy of making changes in order to meet each other's needs. In short, they did the hard work of building an intimate marriage relationship.

Like most couples who choose counseling, Raphael and Joanna met the counselor in both individual and joint sessions. In the individual sessions, the counselor helped them work through personal attitudes and emotions. The counselor helped Joanna deal with the deep emotions she still felt for the other man. She came to understand that these emotions would not subside overnight. Memories of their times together would often flash in her mind, and the desire for the intimacy they shared would often dominate her thinking. Assured by the counselor that her actions did not have to follow these emotions and desires, Joanna continued to work on rebuilding her relationship with Raphael. She chose to say "No, thank you" to the two or three phone calls she received from New York. She knew in her heart that to pursue that relationship was to walk a dead-end street. She knew that Raphael had been faithful to her and that he loved her. Otherwise, he would not be willing to forgive her of her indiscretions. Over a period of about a year, her feelings of intimacy toward Raphael grew, and her feelings and memories of the other man diminished. She knew that she was on the road toward healing.

FORGIVE—AND ASK FOR FORGIVENESS

One of the most difficult times for Joanna came after about nine months of counseling when she began to intensely experience Raphael's love and to understand how deeply she had hurt him. In the early part of counseling, she had focused on his failures and tried to shift the blame of her unfaithfulness to him. But nine months later she knew that she must take responsibility for her own actions. Her guilt weighed heavily on her, and she realized that she had never sincerely asked Raphael for forgiveness.

They both knew that from that point, the past would heal. Now Joanna's sexual unfaithfulness would become only a scar, not an open wound.

Early in the process of recovery, she had intellectually acknowledged that what she did was wrong, and she had asked for forgiveness. But this time she needed his forgiveness on a much deeper level. Now she was keenly aware of her own guilt. Now she understood the gift of forgiveness that Raphael had offered her. She said the words again: "Please forgive me for all the pain I have caused you."

Raphael responded, "I do."

With deep emotion and many tears, they embraced. And they both knew that from that point, the past would heal. Now Joanna's sexual unfaithfulness would become only a scar, not an open wound.

In the early stages of recovery, one of Raphael's deep struggles was living with the awareness that his wife still had strong emotional feelings for another man with whom she had been sexually active. These realities often rained on his parade. He wanted so hard to let the past go, but it was so difficult when he knew that she still had thoughts and feelings for the other man. The counselor assured Raphael that living with this reality was a part of the recovery and that if Joanna denied she had these feelings, the two of them could not build an authentic relationship. The important thing was that Joanna was choosing Raphael over the other man. She was not allowing her emotions to control her actions. He could give thanks for her choices if not for her feelings.

After their night of forgiveness, Raphael knew that his long struggle was over and that Joanna now understood his pain and genuinely regretted all that she had put him through. He knew now that her feelings were for him and that their marriage was going to make it.

For marital healing after unfaithfulness, forgiveness is essential. It involves two key elements: confession and asking for forgiveness on the part of the erring spouse, and genuine forgiveness on the part of the offended spouse. Forgiveness is a promise: "I will no longer hold that against you." Such forgiveness takes place on different emotional levels; thus, Joanna desired to repeat the forgiving process nine months into the counseling session. She included not only her sexual unfaithfulness, but also other failures that came to light as she took an honest look at her marriage relationship.

The counseling continued for several months, but now with an air of confidence rather than the pall of the uncertainty that hung over the early months of recovery. Raphael and Joanna each could now give themselves to the other more fully because trust had been reborn, and they had expressed a new commitment to each other.

When you choose to confess failures, extend forgiveness, and genuinely seek to meet the needs of your spouse, marital intimacy becomes a reality. The elusive dream is no longer elusive or a dream.

However, there is another enemy of marital faithfulness we must address.

PORNOGRAPHY: THE NEW INFIDELITY

With the explosion of pornography on the internet, more couples are facing a different kind of infidelity. It may seem as if pornography has little to do with unfaithfulness. Nonetheless, pornography, when discovered, stimulates many of the same emotions in the spouse as does adultery.

Marsha had been married twenty-three years to Brad. They had three children, and in her words, "had what I thought was a good marriage." She continued, "I knew that we did not have sex as often as we did when we were younger, but when we did, it was good, I thought, for both of us. I guess I was wrong."

One night, Marsha woke up and realized that her husband was not in bed with her. She quietly walked down the hall and saw Brad watching porn in his office. That was the beginning of their estrangement.

Marsha's conclusion is that of many wives when they discover that their husbands are watching porn. "What is wrong with me?" one wife asked. "Why does he go to a screen and watch a woman he doesn't even know? Am I not good enough?" Hurt, anger, repulsion, and feelings of betrayal are common emotions of a wife who discovers that her husband has turned to porn.

Brad's perspective was that porn was just a supplement to his sexual relationship with Marsha. He saw it as a harmless activity that gave him sexual pleasure. "We're both busy. Marsha is a good wife and mother. I don't want to put pressure on her to be more sexual. So, I take care of myself. Why make a big deal of it?"

Marsha saw this as rationalizing inappropriate behavior. In no way did she see it as a light matter. When she found out that it had been going on for two years she was devastated. "He told me that he was not going to get another woman pregnant and that he was not going to get a sexually transmitted disease with pornography, so how could I call that adultery? I call it adultery because he is turning to another woman for sexual pleasure rather than turning to me. The fact that he did it without telling me and denied it until I found the evidence tells me that he knew it was not right."

> "Why does he go to a screen and watch a woman he doesn't even know? Am I not good enough?"

When Brad realized how deeply he had hurt Marsha, he agreed that he would stop, and he did—for a few months. Their relationship seemed to be healing, until eighteen months later Marsha found that indeed he was back on porn sites. That is when she called my office and asked for an appointment.

"I can't go on like this," she said. "I no longer trust him, and I don't want to be sexually intimate with him. I really tried after he told me he would stop. It was hard, but I became more sexually responsive, and we had sex often. I felt like we were making progress, until I discovered the truth. That's when I knew I could not continue playing this game."

I was extremely sympathetic with Marsha. I asked if she thought Brad would talk with me. She said, "He probably would.

I told him this morning that I wanted a divorce, so he knows I'm serious." Brad did come in, and his story was similar to many I have heard through the years. His involvement with pornography began when he was in college and continued through his young adult years. For a brief time in the early years of their marriage, he did not watch porn and told himself that it was a thing of the past. He was in a new stage of life now.

However, the visual images of the past kept popping in his mind, even when he was making love with Marsha. Eventually he fell back into the pattern of watching porn. He never let Marsha know because he knew she would not approve. In his heart, he knew it was wrong, but the pull was too great.

Brad was verbalizing the reality that pornography is addictive, just as addictive as alcohol and drugs. It releases the "happiness" hormone dopamine, just as in a chemical high. In time, it takes more alcohol or harder drugs or more hardcore porn to get the same high. At this stage, the person is addicted. The behavior will not change without treatment. Can the addict find sobriety? Yes, but not without long-term help and accountability.

Brad was not willing to get help. He did not see it as a problem. How many alcoholics have said the same: "I don't have a drinking problem"?

I wish I could say that Brad changed his mind and that he and Marsha were reconciled. But that did not happen. Marsha felt she had done all she could do. She divorced Brad. Brad's attitude toward pornography affected his decision. Even though he knew it was destroying his marriage, he put personal pleasure above marital love.

Why is pornography so detrimental to the marital relationship? Because there is something about the human psyche that cries out for sexual fidelity in marriage. When either the husband or the wife turns elsewhere for sexual fulfillment the spouse is heartbroken. Perhaps this is what Jesus meant when he said that a man who "looks at a woman lustfully has already committed adultery with her in his heart" (Matthew 5:28). It is what some have called mental or emotional adultery. Yes, it differs from physical infidelity, but nonetheless it is adultery.

Can there be reconciliation after infidelity? Yes, but only when there is a willingness from both spouses to take the hard road of repentance and healing.

CHOOSE YOUR RESPONSE TO HURT AND ANGER

I now want to look at some of the common pitfalls that hinder couples in their journey on the road of reality living in the context of infidelity. As noted earlier, discovering your spouse has been sexually unfaithful is like watching a bomb explode in your marriage. Things cannot go on as normal. You must now process new emotions and make some decisions. How you respond to these emotions and decisions will move you toward restoration or divorce.

Most people, when they learn of a spouse's unfaithfulness, are overwhelmed by feelings of hurt and anger. These are deep and powerful emotions. In anger, you could pull the trigger and kill the guilty party, or you could turn and walk out the door and never return. One alternative leads to death, the other to divorce, but neither deals with the issues that gave rise to the unfaithfulness. And both create another whole set of problems with which you must now deal.

Hurt and anger are healthy emotions. They reveal that you are human and that you care about your marriage relationship. They indicate that you see yourself as a valuable person who has been wronged. They reveal your concern for rightness and fairness. You need to process these emotions in a positive way.

Initially, weeping and sobbing are healthy responses to the pain. However, the body is limited in how long it can sustain such agony; thus, sessions of weeping must be interspersed with periods of calm.

Verbally expressing your pain to the unfaithful spouse is a healthy way of processing anger. Be aware that "you" statements tend not only to condemn but also to incite further negative reactions from your spouse. If, for example, you use the following statements, they will tend to incite battle rather than understanding. "You betrayed me . . . you hurt me . . . you took advantage of me . . . you don't love me; you could never have loved me." Such statements place blame and incite negative reactions, while "I" statements simply reveal your emotions.

It is better if you can express your anger with "I" statements rather than "you" statements, which can sound accusing and provoke a defensive or aggressive response. Here are some examples of "I" statements: "I feel betrayed . . . I feel hurt . . . I feel used; I feel taken advantage of . . . I feel that you don't love me; I feel that you could never have loved me . . . I feel unclean . . . I feel like I don't ever want to touch you again."[1] All these statements reveal your thoughts and feelings to your spouse. They are honest, they are not cloaked; they are communicating to your spouse the deep pain you feel. Any recovery requires that your spouse hear and understand the depth of your hurt and anger.

Another way of processing your pain is to share it with a trusted friend, pastor, or counselor. Verbalizing the hurt and anger to another person is a healthy way of working through the anger to a positive resolution.

On the other hand, there are many negative responses to anger that complicate the problem. If in your anger you start throwing glasses and dishes, you may not only physically hurt your spouse and be liable for physical abuse, but you may destroy some of your prized possessions. If this is done in the presence of children, you also give them a visual image of a mother or father out of control. This image is extremely difficult for children to process. Such angry outbursts accompanied by physical threats or actions may land you in jail and further compound your problems. They also alleviate some of the guilt of your spouse; now he can blame you rather than himself because your behavior has demonstrated that you are an unreasonable, uncontrolled person. Removing his guilt or giving him the opportunity to shift the guilt to you is not a part of the recovery process; it pushes your spouse further toward divorce.

Retaliation is another common but very negative response to an unfaithful spouse. Such retaliation may involve going out and having an affair yourself to show your unfaithful spouse what it feels like to be betrayed. Other vengeful tactics are to go to her place of work and cause a scene with angry shouting and yelling. If the unfaithful spouse moves out of the house and continues to see the new partner, a vengeful response would be to drive by their dwelling, throw bricks through a window, call their number and either be silent or sound off, or let the air out of the tires of their cars; or, as in one case I remember, remove the battery from the car. These tactics are juvenile and detrimental as well as being unlawful.

Any effort at revenge is doomed to failure. Returning wrong for wrong simply makes the other person feel less guilty and tends to spark within them the desire to return fire for fire. Thus the problem escalates rather than finds resolution.

SEEK COUNSELING

If your spouse reveals his or her sexual unfaithfulness to you, you will have many questions to answer and many decisions to make.

These questions and decisions are best made with the help of a professional counselor or a trusted friend, who can help both of you think clearly about the best steps to take. Sometimes the erring spouse will not be willing to go for counseling. Then go alone. Start the process. If your spouse is not willing to deal with the situation, you must deal with your own emotions and your own decisions. You are far more likely to make wise decisions if you get the help of someone who is not emotionally involved in the situation.

If you go for counseling, your spouse may eventually join you, even if he or she is reluctant to do so in the beginning. If he or she never joins you, you can walk the road of reality living, and whether or not the marriage is restored, you can live a better life in the future than you have lived in the past.

In my opinion, restoration is the goal toward which you should work when your spouse has been unfaithful. But obviously, restoration is not always possible. Your spouse may be unwilling to break off the sexual liaison or may promise to break it off and in fact continue. Your spouse may actually break off that relationship but later begin another relationship. You cannot make someone deal with their problems, but you can deal with your own problems.

You cannot make someone deal with their problems, but you can deal with your own problems.

The challenge of reality living is to take responsibility for your own thoughts and actions and to seek to do the most constructive thing in life's difficult situations. This is the best approach for your own mental and spiritual health. It has the added possibility of stimulating positive change in the life of your spouse.

FOR FURTHER HELP

- focusonthefamily.com—extensive resources for those impacted by infidelity and/or pornography
- faithfulandtrue.com—for men struggling with sexual addiction and for the wives who need support and counsel

The Alcoholic/ Drug-Abusing Spouse

Few things damage marital intimacy more than alcoholism. We have all known families torn by alcoholism, marriages broken, lives shattered. Perhaps we grew up in such a home—or are struggling with an alcoholic spouse right now. If so, we know only too well that alcoholism is a family problem.[1] The drinking and subsequent behavior of the alcoholic harms not only the life of the alcoholic but also the lives of all who interact with him or her.

But how do you know your spouse might be an alcoholic? Researchers define alcoholism as "a disease that includes the following four symptoms:

- craving—a strong need, or urge, to drink;
- loss of control—not being able to stop drinking once drinking has begun;

- physical dependence—withdrawal symptoms, such as nausea, sweating, shakiness, and anxiety after stopping drinking; and
- tolerance—the need to drink greater amounts of alcohol to get high."[2]

In a 2015 study, it was reported that 56.9 percent of Americans aged eighteen and older indicated having had an alcoholic beverage within the last month.[3]

Since alcohol is the most widely used and most readily available drug,[4] we will focus most of our attention in this chapter on what alcoholism does to a marriage.

Why is alcohol so destructive to the marital relationship? The answer lies in the behavior that grows out of substance abuse. The substance abuser lives in an egocentric world. In a general sense, that is true of all of us, but it is profoundly true of the substance abuser. The abuser of alcohol—or of drugs—is inwardly directed and absorbed with his own pain or pleasure and thus has a very self-centered life. This self-centeredness impairs his normal day-to-day living and his personal relationships. The pattern of behavior brings destructive traits to the marital relationship.

What are these destructive traits? The most serious is dishonesty. In her effort to hide her addiction, the abuser becomes a master of deceit. Such deceit is the antithesis of intimacy. It builds walls between marital partners. Other aspects of the alcoholic behavioral pattern include an unwillingness to face conflict, emotional distance from the marriage partner, lack of empathy, and what appears to be a disinterest in the spouse. The addict's addiction makes her insensitive to the feelings of those who care for her. The addict's highest priority in life is using the addicting substance. She will stop at nothing to feed the addiction. Even though she knows that her use of drugs or alcohol causes her spouse (and children) untold suffering, she keeps drinking and is willing to let her family suffer.

While under the influence, addicts often engage in behaviors that ultimately destroy the marriage. Acts of sexual infidelity are characteristic of alcoholics. The fact that a husband was drunk at the time is little consolation to a grief-stricken wife. Physical and emotional neglect and abuse are also characteristic of those under the influence. Even when he is not abusive, his talk and behavior may evoke disgust, pity, anger, and fear in the heart of the spouse. Add to that having problems at work/being unable to hold down a job; driving under the influence and putting both loved ones and strangers at risk; financial irresponsibility; alienating family and friends; doing physical harm to oneself to the point of possibly shortening one's life . . . all these can wreak irrevocable harm on a marriage. Life with a substance abuser makes marital intimacy seem impossible.

> *Life with a substance abuser makes marital intimacy seem impossible.*

BARBARA: "I WANT TO LOVE HIM, BUT . . . "

Barbara knew the sense of hopelessness that comes from living with an alcoholic husband. She shared with me that her husband, Dan, drank some before they got married, but after marriage his drinking became a bigger part of his life. For the past ten years, his alcoholism had been tearing their marriage apart. Seeing her husband drunk was hard enough for Barbara, but the verbal abuse that Dan inflicted on her when he was under the influence of alcohol made the situation almost unbearable. This was compounded by the fact that his alcoholism made it difficult for him to hold a job. Dan's pattern was to start a new job, express his excitement about it, and renew his commitment to be a success this time. But such hope was always short-lived. He would return to drinking and then lose his job. After each job loss, he would go on a drinking binge, followed by a drying-out period and then a new job search. A new job led to new hope, but the drinking would resume, and the cycle would begin again.

Barbara learned to tell where they were in the cycle. She also knew what was coming next. She really did not want a divorce. But things had only gotten worse, despite her religious faith and her talks with Dan about the problem.

"I'm to the point that I don't know what to do now. I find my love feelings for Dan dying. I want to respect him. I want to love him. I want to help him, but I don't know how," she said. Ten years seemed like an eternity, and Barbara was thinking seriously of the one thing she had never wanted—divorce.

Understand enabling behavior

In talking further with Barbara, I found that in many ways she was the classic enabler. Unwittingly, she had helped Dan continue his addictive lifestyle. Her father was an alcoholic, which is often the case with wives who find themselves married to alcoholics. In childhood, she had learned the skills of overlooking disruptive behavior, trying to keep peace in the family, excusing her father's behavior, and longing for the day when things would be different. Barbara now used these unconscious skills to foster Dan's alcoholism.

The enabler feels compelled to try at all costs to clean up the chaos that the alcohol or drug use produces. In so doing, he or she only perpetuates the addiction. Without an enabler, it would be difficult for the user to continue the habit. The enabler often feels anger but manages to hide it with genuine concern for the other person. The enabler is patient and unselfish and often over-protects and tries to rescue the substance abuser. The payoff is a shallow peace that cannot lead to marital intimacy.

I knew that if Barbara were ever to become an agent of positive change in her marriage, she would have to adjust her thinking and her behavior. She would have to learn to give up the responsibility of her husband's behavior and accept responsibility for her own be-havior. She would have to let Dan suffer the consequences of his addictive lifestyle. For many spouses of substance abusers, this will require a fundamental change of behavior. The spouse must recognize that the only thing that ultimately will moti-vate a substance abuser to make the decision to get off drugs

Trying to be loving and supportive of the drug addict in a caretaking manner only makes the situation worse.

and seek treatment is suffering the consequences of his lifestyle. When this happens, the abuser may realize that to continue in that lifestyle is to lose everything that is important to him. This realization most often comes as the result of a crisis. This may be the loss of a job, severe illness, an arrest, the separation of a spouse, or the rejection of family and friends. It is only when the addict comes to despise his own lifestyle that he or she will be motivated to seek treatment.

Barbara had come to me for marital counseling, but I knew that such counseling would be fruitless unless we addressed her husband's addiction. My first suggestion was that Barbara begin attending the local Al-Anon chapter. Al-Anon is a national organization that provides information and support to family members of substance abusers. It offers them the practical insights and the emotional support to become agents of positive change. They come to realize that although they cannot control the addicted behavior of their loved one, they can influence him.[5]

Alcoholism and other addictions tend to isolate families. Shame, uncertainty, and fear of the unknown often paralyze the spouse into inactivity. What Barbara learned at Al–Anon was that she was not alone. Millions of men and women are married to alcoholics who have experienced a similar history in their own marriages. Their lives also have become unmanageable.

But Barbara also found hope at Al-Anon. The first step was to accept responsibility for her own attitudes and actions, which echoed the first two principles of reality living. The second step was to let Dan accept responsibility for his actions. She learned that she did not cause his drinking; she could not control it, nor could she cure it. She learned that trying to be loving and supportive of the drug addict in a caretaking manner only makes the situation worse. She learned that drug addiction causes one to regress emotionally, to become extremely immature, and that alcoholics learn how to manipulate, con, and lie in order to be successful addicts. Their stories and excuses sound so plausible that the spouse is inclined to believe them.

BARBARA LEARNS TOUGH LOVE

Barbara learned how to admit the truth that Dan had used her all these years to continue his addictive behavior. She admitted her imperfections in enabling his behavior, although she did not blame herself for his addiction. It was now time for her to refuse to be his pawn and to become a strong pillar of tough love. She learned how to love Dan genuinely by refusing to pick up the pieces, to make excuses, or to rescue him from the consequences of his behavior. She learned that she was responsible for her own attitude toward his drinking, and also that he was responsible for his own behavior. Barbara realized that she did not have to get caught up in Dan's roller-coaster behavior. She also realized that she could not change him. She could, however, seek to influence him through tough love.

She remembers well the difficulty of letting him stay in the local jail in spite of his pleadings for her to get him out. She called a friend from Al-Anon. They prayed and cried together on the telephone. The thought of Dan spending the night in jail was extremely painful for Barbara, but she knew that her refusal to bail him out was her strongest expression of love at the moment and that love is the most powerful weapon for good.

Over the next year, she watched Dan lose his job, knowing that if she had jumped in and helped as she used to, she could have saved his job. But she realized that something more important was at stake here than saving Dan's job; namely, helping him accept responsibility for his own behavior.

After Dan lost his job, he went on another drinking binge. This is when Barbara took the two children and moved in with her mother.

This was the last straw for Dan. He came begging and pleading for Barbara to return. He promised that he would never drink again, that he had learned his lesson. With the support of her friends at Al-Anon, she was able to say no to Dan's tears. She would not return until he entered a treatment program, and even then she would not return until they had marriage counseling.

There would be no more fast fixes. Unless Dan would deal with his alcoholism and unless he were willing to work with her on learning how to build a good marriage, she would never return.

Dan came back the next night and begged for Barbara's return. He would go to treatment if she would just return. Barbara recognized this as a further attempt to manipulate her. Her response was a kind, firm no.

"I love you too much to return to you now," she told him. "I will not short-circuit the process. If I return, it will be after you have dealt with your alcoholism and after we have dealt with our marital problems." She told him of a treatment program in a nearby city and assured him that she would work with him on getting into the program, that, in fact, she and the children would come on occasion for counseling sessions with him at the treatment center's request.

"Dan, we have a serious problem," she continued. "It is not going to go away by itself. We all need help. This is your chance to decide if you want your marriage and family, or if you want to live with alcohol for the rest of your life."

Within three days, Dan was in the treatment center, and for the next three months, he entered a whole new world; a world of reality; a world where people accepted responsibility for their own actions and emotions; a world where people learned to understand themselves and the value of relating to others. He learned about alcoholism, but he also learned more about himself. For the first time in his life, Dan began to realize that life in the real world could be much more satisfying than life in the delusional world of alcohol.

At the end of the ninety-day treatment program (in which Barbara and the children also participated under the direction of their counselor), Dan was released with the full understanding that he and Barbara would not be living together until they had received sufficient marriage counseling to heal the emotional hurts of the past ten years and to build new patterns of relating to each other in marriage. This time, Dan was not begging for Barbara to return. He was living in the real world and knew that he had deeply hurt her with his self-centered, destructive behavior over the past ten years and that he had to allow time for her healing. He also recognized that he had a great deal to learn about how to relate to his wife and his children.

I began extensive marriage and family counseling with Dan and Barbara and their children, which nine months later resulted in Barbara and the children moving back home. Dan continued to attend Alcoholics Anonymous (AA)[6] meetings once a week during the time of our marriage counseling. Barbara likewise saw her need for personal growth and continued her weekly meetings with her friends in Al-Anon. Dan had only one brief relapse during the nine months. He was at a business meeting and thought that he could have a drink socially without getting drunk. One drink led to two and before the evening was over, Dan had to be taken home in a taxi. The next week he went to AA meetings each day and shared his relapse with his AA support group. He also shared this information with Barbara and later with me in our counseling session.

This openness was far different from his previous style of denial and lying. Barbara and Dan both had a high level of confidence that their marriage would be vastly different from the past ten years. I continued to see them monthly for the first six months after they moved back together and semiannually for two years after that.

As of this writing, it's been five years since I last counseled with Barbara and Dan, but every Christmas I've received a card and a brief note recounting some of the events of the year. Always they express their gratitude.

> *The fact is that most addicts do not change—until their personal pain becomes unbearable.*

Barbara and Dan's story is one of success. (There is success but never a cure. An alcoholic is always only one drink away from the addiction.) Unfortunately, their story is also a rarity. Most spouses married to substance abusers end up divorcing them. They have tried sensible conversation, angry lectures, silent withdrawal, crying, pleading, trying to save face, making excuses, picking up the pieces, and hoping against hope that their spouses will change.

The fact is that most addicts do not change—until their personal pain becomes so intense that it is unbearable. This pain may come from any of the natural consequences of their addiction, such as loss of job, physical illness, rejection of friends. But the deepest pain that an addict can experience is the thought of losing a spouse or some other deeply significant person in his life. That is what motivated Dan to seek treatment, and that is what motivates most addicts to seek treatment. The thought of losing the one person who means the most to them in the whole world is enough pain to motivate many addicts to reach out for help.

This means that the spouse or good friend must be strong enough not to cave in to the initial manipulation of the alcoholic, but must stand kindly but firmly for the necessary long-term treatment, which includes follow-up meetings with AA or another appropriate support group. Most spouses and good friends will not be strong enough to take this reality-living approach without the guidance and support of a group such as Al-Anon. After all, most of these people have a ten- or fifteen-year record of being an enabler. These patterns do not change easily. Even when the spouse begins to practice tough love, well-meaning friends and family may accuse him or her of abandoning the alcoholic. Thus, the first positive step that any family member of an alcoholic can take is to become a part of an educational support group such as Al-Anon.

KNOW ABOUT PROGRAMS FOR SUBSTANCE ABUSERS

Another significant step in the process of becoming an agent of positive change in a marriage with a substance abuser is to discover the treatment center options available so that when the time comes that your spouse is willing to go for treatment, you will be ready to suggest a treatment center.

There are three basic formats for treating drug abusers. One is *outpatient therapy*. The outpatient program typically provides a time for detoxification if needed, weekly meetings, individual and group counseling, peer counseling, and frequent urine drug screening. Peer counseling and urine screening are extremely important. The addict cannot con other addicts. Knowing that he or she is going to be tested for drugs is a strong deterrent and motivates the drug user to say no to temptation. Outpatient programs are less expensive and less disruptive to one's work and family relationships. They work best with people who are in good health and have a strong desire to become substance-free.

Inpatient treatment is a more intensive program. It usually involves detoxification, educational training, group and individual therapy, family involvement, and sometimes occupational and recreational therapy. Such a program may last six weeks to three months and at the end introduces the patient to Alcoholics

Anonymous or to some other follow-up group. Inpatient treatment has the advantage of being intensive and removes the drug user from both the drug and the drug-using environment. Those who have been addicted for a long period of time, or are in poor health, or are in a living environment that encourages drug use usually need an inpatient program.

A third approach to treating the substance abuser is a *residential program*. These programs offer long-term treatment in a controlled environment where the recovering substance user can learn how to live without drugs. Residential programs usually run from six months to a year. They utilize a very structured program, keeping the patient constructively busy and away from drugs and drug-using friends. The residential program usually offers dormitory-style living, daily responsibilities in caring for the facility, family style meals, and a fairly disciplined environment. Usually, such programs include educational and vocational training along with group activities. Typically, counseling focuses not only on treating drug abuse but also on dealing with any underlying emotional/relational problems. Residential programs are more commonly used with adolescents or young adults than with older adults. Such programs can be expensive. Medical insurance may or may not pay for such treatment.

Certain drug treatment programs have had more success than others—success being defined as drug-free living accompanied by responsible living and positive, growing relationships after the treatment. The most successful treatment programs are characterized by the following elements: (1) a commitment to a drug-free environment and a goal of total abstinence, (2) competent medical and nursing care, (3) a strong emphasis on one's personal spiritual life, (4) educational sessions that provide understanding of the effects of drugs, (5) both group and individual therapy sessions, (6) involvement of the larger family (spouse, children, or others) in the treatment process, and (7) a strong commitment to getting the patient into a support group after the initial treatment program. You can find information on available treatment centers through your Al–Anon support group, a local counselor or pastor, your local mental health clinic, or by talking with friends.[7] It is always advisable to learn as much about a treatment program as possible early in the process so that when your spouse is ready for treatment, you will be ready with a viable suggestion. Most treatment programs welcome visits and are happy to discuss with family members their methods and costs of treatments. Costs vary greatly among treatment programs. Most health insurance programs have provision for addiction treatment. You should be aware of all these details long before your spouse is willing to go for treatment.

The most common mistake of an individual married to a substance abuser is to hope that the situation will simply take care of itself, that the abuser will wake up one morning and decide to stop her addictive behavior. The reality is that this almost never happens. When one is truly addicted, it is not a matter of simply deciding to get off the drug. At this point, the body has a physical addiction to the drug and will drive the addict incessantly to meet that need. Once addicted, the substance abuser will need outside help to break the destructive habit.

The role of the spouse who would be an agent of positive change is to let the abuser experience the results of his or her own abuse. The sooner the abuser comes to the end of the rope, the sooner he will reach out for help. It often takes years for the disease of alcoholism to disable the addict physically to the point that nonfamily members are aware there is a problem. Long before that, the spouse knows and needs to love enough to confront the reality of the disease.

If you are married to a substance-abusing spouse, you must

Research has made it abundantly clear that the most successful treatment programs are those that point the individual to the help and power of God.

insist that the use of alcohol or drugs and its resultant behavior is not acceptable. Things cannot go on as usual. When you affirm by your actions that you will no longer make excuses nor get the abuser off the hook, you are doing the good work of tough love. You have now increased the likelihood of your spouse's deciding to seek treatment. Without this tough-love approach, the likelihood of your substance-abusing spouse making a change is almost nil.

Finally, don't ignore the important role of the spiritual life both for the abuser and the caring spouse in overcoming the addiction. Research has made it abundantly clear that the most successful treatment programs are those programs that point the individual to the help and power of God. In fact, the first two steps of the Alcoholic Anonymous Twelve-Step program recognize that we are helpless to change without God.[8] Many alcoholics who had no spiritual reference points earlier find themselves calling for divine help and benefiting from that call. The addict is helpless to change himself, but with the help of God, no addict is hopeless.

As for the spouse who is seeking to be an agent of positive change, the pain of observing an addicted mate often seems overwhelming. Your sense of isolation from friends and family may cause you to feel alone. You too need the help of God and His representatives—fellow humans who love, care, and are knowledgeable about how to relate redemptively to those who are addicted. The most important step you can take is to pray for God's guidance and then call a friend, pastor, counselor, or a local Al–Anon group.

With the support of God and others, you can put reality-living principles into practice with a substance-abusing spouse. In this case, tough love is the most powerful weapon for good. It is only this love that will truly help the alcoholic or drug-abusing spouse.

FOR FURTHER HELP

- celebraterecovery.com
- findtreatment.samhsa.gov—for help in choosing a treatment facility. Or check with your local Al-Anon chapter
- nar-anon.org—for families of those struggling with narcotics addiction
- Co-Dependents Anonymous (CoDA.org)—for those who, like Barbara, are dealing with "enabling" behaviors

A FINAL WORD:
There's Hope

It will be obvious by now that this is not a book for casual reading. It is a book to ponder—and act on. The issues discussed have enormous consequences on marriage and family in particular and on society at large.

This book calls for action. It is my hope that this book will jolt the passive reader in a desperate marriage into reality and urge you to take steps that hold the potential of creating positive change in your marriage.

The people you have met in these pages may not represent your situation perfectly, but I hope they are close enough for you to have identified with their pain. I hope their stories have challenged you to take a fresh look at your marriage. I understand that this may be difficult, especially if you have lived in a hard marriage for a long time. But you know well that time alone does not heal the troublesome behaviors we have described in this book. Perhaps this knowledge will encourage you to take a new approach.

We have looked extensively at the myths many of us believe and live by—and the six "realities" that counter those myths and can lead to positive and lasting change in a hard marriage. We've seen how using the five love languages is key to enhancing communication with our spouse.

I do not wish to minimize your pain. You are walking a difficult road, one that requires courage and compassion. You may well find that you need to apply tough love to your situation—as we have already seen in the stories shared in this book.

The journey toward becoming an agent for positive change in your marriage begins by saying no to the four commonly held myths discussed in chapter 1. As long as you allow these myths to hold you in bondage, you will never be able to take the positive steps of reality living.

Let me review these myths and ask you to answer two questions:

Have I believed these myths in the past?

Will I continue to believe these myths in the future?

If your answer to the first question is yes, I hope your answer to the second question will be no.

THE MYTHS

1. My environment determines my state of mind. Have you fallen into the trap of believing that your happiness is determined by your spouse's behavior?

2. People cannot change. Have you allowed yourself to become discouraged by believing that your spouse will never change his or her troublesome behavior?

3. In a desperate marriage, I have only two options—resigning myself to a life of misery or getting out of the marriage. Have you allowed yourself to become sidetracked by obsessing over the question, "How can I get out of this marriage and get on with my life?" Or have you been sidetracked by yielding to the conclusion, "My life is miserable, but there's nothing I can do about it"? Neither of these sidetracks will lead you to the destination of an intimate marriage.

4. Some situations are hopeless—and my situation is one of these. Have you also concluded that your situation falls into this category—hopeless? To believe this myth is to underestimate the power of your own potential. It creates a defeatist attitude within you that stifles positive motivation.

Perhaps you have believed one or more of these myths in the past. I hope that the stories in this book have helped you understand that these myths are untrue. Your environment does not determine your happiness. Your spouse's behavior cannot keep you from living a happy, fulfilled life. People can change and often do when properly motivated. A person in a desperate marriage has more than the two options of divorce or misery. Because we are human, we have the capacity for change. When we change the way we think and behave, the situation changes.

Refusing to believe these commonly held myths prepares you to become an agent for positive change in your marriage by applying the principles of reality living. Once more, let's review these principles.

THE REALITIES

1. I am responsible for my own attitude. This reality affirms that you are responsible for your own state of mind. Attitude has to do with the way you choose to think about things. This reality allows you to refuse to believe the myths we have discussed above. You are free to choose what you will believe. You can believe that your marriage is hopeless, or you can believe that "there has got to be a way to turn this marriage in a positive direction." You choose your own attitudes.

2. My attitude affects my actions. The reason attitudes are so important is that they affect your actions. By actions, I mean your behavior and words. If you have a pessimistic, defeatist, negative attitude, you will express it in negative words and behavior. If you choose to think optimistically, it will show up in your words and behavior. You may not be able to control your environment, but you can control the way you think about your environment, and your attitude will affect your behavior.

3. I cannot change others, but I can influence others. You probably believe that you cannot change your spouse, but you may often overlook the fact that you can and do influence your spouse. Because we are relational creatures, we are all influenced by the words and behavior of those around us.

You cannot force your spouse to change what you consider to be undesirable behavior, but by your words and your behavior you can influence your spouse in a positive direction. All of society is built on this reality. Exerting your influence on your spouse has tremendous potential for stimulating positive change in a desperate marriage.

4. My emotions do not control my actions. Emotions are the spontaneous feelings we experience as we encounter life. However, human beings are more than emotions. Emotions stimulate us to take action, but we must temper our emotions with our thoughts and our desires. Otherwise, negative emotions will always lead to negative actions.

For example, if you acknowledge that you are angry about your spouse's behavior but you have a desire to build an intimate marriage, you conclude that you will first ask, "What motivated my spouse to the behavior that made me angry? What is going on inside of him, and what would be my most productive response to his behavior?"

Tempering your emotions with your thoughts and desires will more likely lead you to take constructive actions. Your emotions need not control your actions.

5. Admitting my imperfections does not mean that I am a failure. None of us is perfect. You may have concluded that the major problem in your marriage is your spouse's troublesome behavior. Even if this is true, it does not mean that your behavior is above reproach. Often, the first step in becoming an agent of positive change in your marriage is to acknowledge that your own behavior in the past has been inappropriate. Acknowledging this to yourself and to your spouse may prepare the way for a more positive approach in the future.

Admitting your own imperfections does not mean that you bear all the responsibility for your desperate marriage. It simply means that you are willing to accept responsibility for your own improper actions. Taking such responsibility does not mean that you are a failure, but rather it is a sign of your maturity.

6. Love is the most powerful weapon for good in the world. Meeting your spouse's emotional need for love has the greatest potential for stimulating positive change in his or her behavior. Since love is our deepest emotional need, the person who meets that need will have the greatest influence on our lives.

Perhaps in the past you have not been loving in your words and behavior toward your spouse. Most likely this is because your spouse's behavior has not stirred warm, loving feelings toward him or her. Thus, you must return to reality number four and realize that you need not allow your emotions to control your actions. You can love your spouse even though you may not have warm feelings toward him or her.

Remember, love is not essentially a feeling; it is a way of thinking and behaving. Love is the attitude that says, "I choose to look out for your interests. How may I help you?" This attitude will lead you to loving actions. Such actions, in turn, meet your spouse's emotional need for love and stimulate positive emotions inside him or her, making it easier for him or her to reciprocate your love.

Remember also that we all have basic needs. Seek to meet your spouse's basic needs.

Understanding and speaking the primary love language of your spouse will also make this process much more effective. It will help your spouse feel loved.

THE 5 LOVE LANGUAGES

Words of Affirmation
Verbally affirming your spouse for the good things he or she does

Quality Time
Giving your spouse undivided attention

Receiving Gifts
Presenting a gift to your spouse that says, "I was thinking about you."

Acts of Service
Doing something for your spouse that is meaningful to him or her

Physical Touch
Kissing, embracing, patting on the back, holding hands, having sexual intercourse

If your loving acts do not produce positive changes within your desperate marriage, then perhaps it is time for tough love. We have shared many examples of tough love in the preceding chapters. Remember, tough love is no less love. In fact, it may be the only kind of love your spouse can receive. It may be even more difficult to express than tender love. In expressing such tough love, you may have to go against the emotion of fear of what your spouse will do when you take such loving action. Again, reality living reminds you that your emotions need not control your actions. Love asks the question, "What is the best thing I can do for my spouse?" Tender or tough, love is the most powerful weapon for good in the world.

Applying the six principles of reality living to your marriage may be the most difficult thing you have ever done, but I can assure you that it holds the greatest potential for the well-being of your marriage.

Reality living means that you refuse to believe your situation is hopeless. You choose, rather, to believe in the power of human potential for change and to recognize that all of us are influenced daily by those who are part of our lives. The more intimate the relationship, the greater the influence.

Thus, the marriage relationship holds tremendous potential for influencing a spouse to make positive changes. The key is in learning how best to exert this influence. I sincerely hope that this book will help guide you toward becoming an effective agent for positive change in your marriage.

As you use this book and walk this road, you may well need the help and encouragement of a friend, pastor, or counselor. It is always a sign of maturity to reach out for help. We were not made to live in isolation. We reach our highest potential when we work together in community. You may wish to share this book with your therapist and let him or her help you apply these insights to your life and marriage.

If, in applying the principles of reality living to your marriage, you experience significant growth, or if you and your spouse overcome the troublesome barriers that we have discussed in this book, please share your story with others. Telling your story may encourage others in a desperate marriage to reach out for help.

If we can all be more open about our marital struggles and the steps we are taking to stimulate positive change, we can create a climate of hope, which contemporary society clearly needs. If you share your story and I share my story, together we can make a difference in the world.

Notes

Chapter 1. The Valley of Pain

1. Jen Abbas, *Generation Ex: Adult Children of Divorce and the Healing of Our Pain* (Little Rock, Ark.: Family Life, 2006), 1.

Chapter 2. Where You Start: Attitudes and Actions

1. Philippians 4:6–8.
2. Ephesians 5:25. According to the biblical writers, Jesus Christ's death by crucifixion was done willingly to pay for the sins of men and women. It was an act of sacrificial love to bring estranged men and women back to God. See Matthew 16:21; John 10:17–18; Romans 5:6–10.
3. Titus 2:4.
4. For a fuller explanation of this concept, see Gary Chapman, *The 5 Love Languages: The Secret to Love That Lasts* (Chicago: Northfield, 2015).

Chapter 3. Why Did He Do That?

1. William Glasser, *Take Charge of Your Life: How to Get What You Need with Choice-Theory Psychology* (Bloomington, IN: iUniverse, 2013), 5.
2. George Sweeting, *Who Said That?* (Chicago: Moody, 1995), 209.

Chapter 6. The Depressed Spouse

1. Jacqueline M. Thielen, M.D., "Premenstrual dysphoric disorder: Different from PMS?," Mayo Clinic, November 14, 2015, https://www.mayoclinic.org/diseases-conditions/premenstrual-syndrome/expert-answers/pmdd/faq-20058315.
2. "Depression During Pregnancy and Postpartum," www.postpartum.net/learn-more/depression-during-pregnancy-postpartum/.
3. Two excellent resources on the causes and treatment of depression are David B. Biebel and Harold G. Koenig, *New Light on Depression* (Grand Rapids: Zondervan, 2003); and Frank Minirth and Paul Meier, *Happiness Is a Choice* (Grand Rapids: Baker Books, 2013).
4. In particular, see H. Norman Wright, *Recovering from the Losses of Life* (Grand Rapids: Revell, 2006).

Chapter 7. The Controlling Spouse

1. An excellent resource for responding to someone who wants to control your time, energy, and even your love is Henry Cloud and John Townsend's book *Boundaries* (Grand Rapids: Zondervan, 1992); see also their sequel, *Boundaries*

in Marriage (Grand Rapids: Zondervan, 2002), especially chapter 4, "It Takes Two to Make One."

Chapter 8. The Verbally Abusive Spouse

1. Proverbs 29:11.
2. Proverbs 18:21.
3. See Hebrews 12:5–7.

Chapter 9. The Physically Abusive Spouse

1. "Understanding Intimate Partner Violence, Fact Sheet 2014," Centers for Disease Control and Prevention, National Center for Injury Prevention and Control; https://stacks.cdc.gov/view/cdc/31068. An "intimate partner" includes current and former spouses and dating partners.
2. Rachael Revesz, "National Domestic Violence Awareness Month: Around 4,000 women have died from domestic violence in the past year," *Independent*, October 1, 2016, http://www.independent.co.uk/news/world/americas/women-national-domestic-violence-awareness-month-october-death-murder-abuse-a7341121.html.
3. "Intimate Partner Violence in the United States," U.S. Department of Justice, Bureau of Justice Statistics (December 28, 2006); http://www.ojp.gov/bjs/intimate/ipv.htm; and "Domestic violence against women: Recognize patterns, seek help" at https://www.mayoclinic.org/healthy-lifestyle/adult-health/in-depth/domestic-violence/art-20048397.
4. "Intimate Partner Violence in the United States: Circumstances"; https://www.bjs.gov/content/pub/pdf/ipvus.pdf.
5. Helene Henderson, *Domestic Violence and Child Abuse Sourcebook*, ed. (Detroit: Omnigraphics, 2000), 50–51.
6. "Intimate Partner Violence in the U.S.," U.S. Department of Justice, Bureau of Justice Statistics.
7. Henderson, *Domestic Violence and Child Abuse Sourcebook*, 50.
8. In addition, she can read more about the subject of physical abuse. Here's an excellent resource that can be found on the internet to help you recognize and deal with an abusive spouse: "Domestic violence against women: Recognize patterns, seek help" at https://www.mayoclinic.org/healthy-lifestyle/adult-health/in-depth/domestic-violence/art-20048397.
9. Robert S. McGee, *The Search for Significance* (Nashville: Nelson, 1998).

Chapter 10. The Sexually Abusive/Sexually Abused Spouse

1. Cynthia Kubetin and James Mallory, *Beyond the Darkness: Healing for Victims of Sexual Abuse* (Dallas: Word, 1992).
2. "Fact Sheet: Sexual Abuse of Boys," Prevent Child Abuse America (Chicago, 2007); at http://www.preventchildabuse.org, under "Research: Child Abuse and Neglect."
3. Marianne Barrett, Robin J. Wilson, and Carmen Long, "Measuring Motiva-

tion to Change in Sexual Offenders from Institutional Intake to Community Treatment," *Sexual Abuse: A Journal of Research and Treatment* 15, no. 4 (October 2003): 269–83.

4. An excellent resource for understanding and responding to sexual abuse and its impact on marriage is Victoria L. Johnson, *Children and Sexual Abuse* (Downers Grove, Ill.: InterVarsity, 2007).

Chapter 11. The Uncommunicative Spouse

1. Psalm 7:11 KJV.
2. See Matthew 26:37.

Chapter 12. The Unfaithful Spouse

1. Depending on one's personality, an offended spouse may feel many different responses. It is perfectly acceptable to say any of the following to convey your frustration or anger: "I feel like I am going to suffocate . . . I feel like I wish I could die . . . I feel like I could kill that other person . . . I feel like I could kill you . . . I am so confused; I don't understand . . . I thought we had a good marriage . . . I feel like I have failed you . . . I feel like I want you to leave; I feel like I want to get out of here."

Chapter 13. The Alcoholic/Drug-Abusing Spouse

1. Al-Anon statement of purpose: http://www.alanon-nassau-ny.org/alanon.htm.
2. Amy L. Sutton, *Alcoholism Sourcebook*, ed. 2nd ed., (Detroit: Omnigraphics, 2007), 17.
3. "Results from the 2015 National Survey on Drug Use and Health: Detailed Tables," Substance Abuse and Mental Health Services Administration (SAMHSA), https://www.samhsa.gov/data/sites/default/files/NSDUH-DetTabs-2015/NSDUH-DetTabs-2015/NSDUH-DetTabs-2015.htm#tab2-41b.
4. "Substance Abuse: The Nation's Number One Health Problem," Schneider Institute for Health Policy, Brandeis University, Waltham. Mass., 2001, 11; see https://www.ncjrs.gov/pdffiles1/ojjdp/fs200117.pdf.
5. Learn more about Al-Anon at al-anon.org.
6. Learn more about Alcoholic Anonymous at http://www.aa.org.
7. A very helpful internet address in choosing a treatment facility is https://findtreatment.samhsa.gov/, which has the list "A Quick Guide to Finding Effective Alcohol and Drug Addiction Treatment," Substance Abuse and Mental Health Services Administration. Another helpful website that will help to identify whether your spouse is an alcoholic is "Are You Troubled by Someone's Drinking," Al-Anon/Alateen, at https://al-anon.org/pdf/S17.pdf.
8. The first two steps of the Twelve Steps of Alcoholics Anonymous are: 1. We admitted we were powerless over alcohol—that our lives had become unmanageable. 2. Came to believe that a Power greater than ourselves could restore us to sanity; see http://www.aa.org/.

Acknowledgments

I am deeply indebted to the couples who have allowed me to be a part of their journey toward loving solutions in their desperate marriages. For some, the journey has been extremely long and painful. For others, solutions came easier and earlier. For all, it has been a road of growth and discovery. I am privileged to have walked the road with these people and now to tell their stories. I dedicate this book to them.

My appreciation to Tricia Kube, my administrative assistant for more than twenty years. Tricia not only computerized the manuscript but offered many helpful suggestions. Jim Vincent was of immense help in polishing the original manuscript. My thanks also to Betsey Newenhuyse, who developed and updated this current edition.

As always, I want to express my love and appreciation for Karolyn, my wife for more than fifty years. Her joyful spirit is a constant source of encouragement to me.

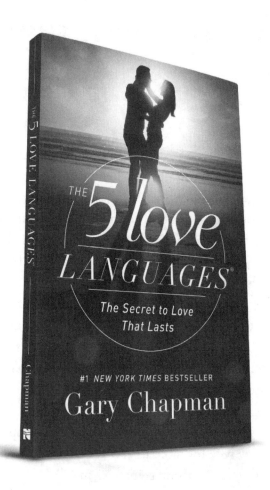